THE WISE HAZEL TREE

RITUALS FOR LIVING IN SEASON

CAROLANN GREGOIRE, MSW

BALBOA
PRESS

A DIVISION OF HAY HOUSE

Balboa Press books may be ordered through booksellers or by contacting:

Balboa Press
A Division of Hay House
1663 Liberty Drive
Bloomington, IN 47403
www.balboapress.com
1 (877) 407-4847

Because of the dynamic nature of the Internet, any web addresses or links contained in this book may have changed since publication and may no longer be valid. The views expressed in this work are solely those of the author and do not necessarily reflect the views of the publisher, and the publisher hereby disclaims any responsibility for them.

The author of this book does not dispense medical advice or prescribe the use of any technique as a form of treatment for physical, emotional, or medical problems without the advice of a physician, either directly or indirectly. The intent of the author is only to offer information of a general nature to help you in your quest for emotional and spiritual well-being. In the event you use any of the information in this book for yourself, which is your constitutional right, the author and the publisher assume no responsibility for your actions.

Any people depicted in stock imagery provided by Getty Images are models,
and such images are being used for illustrative purposes only.
Certain stock imagery © Getty Images.

ISBN: 978-1-9822-0237-8 (sc)
ISBN: 978-1-9822-0236-1 (e)

Library of Congress Control Number: 2018904615

Print information available on the last page.

Balboa Press rev. date: 09/11/2018

Table of Contents

Acknowledgments vii

Author's Note ix

Introduction xi

All is Well in the Fall of the Leaves xii

An Autumn Essay xiii

September~ Celebrate Accomplishments 1

October~ Honor the Dead 13

November~ Express Gratitude for Life's Bounty 28

All is Well in the Stillness of her Womb 42

A Winter Essay 43

December~ Trust the Sun's Return 44

January~ Rest With the Soul 61

February~ Welcome Your Bliss 82

All is Well Under Spring's Enchantment 100

A Spring Poem and Essay 101

March~ Implant Ideas 103

April~ Tend the Soil 120

May~ Discover the Divine Feminine 134

All Is Well in the Shade of the Tree 154

A Summer Essay 155

June~ Nurture New Life 157

July~ Foster Growth 176

August~ Prepare to Harvest 191

Appendix 205

Guide for Ritual Making 206

Glossary 211

Suggested Reading 219

Acknowledgments

My husband, Tom who listened constructively to the book all hours of the day and night.

Chrissy, my editor, her patient tutoring on the art of
continuity, flow and the correct use of commas.

My petites, Paul, Kari, Eric, Phil and Jesse's endless supply of pride, joy and love.

My inspiring muses:

Tom, Kim, Jorie, Cindy, Donna, Chrissy, Kathy, Corie, Dianna,
Molly, Tahlia, the Griffins, Emma, Mom and Grandma

The YaYas' unbridled enthusiasm.

Sister Sharon's artistic eye

Nature's clock, Walhalla Ravine.

A special thank you to my incredibly talented nephew, Ryan Troy Ford who illustrated
the book, drawing the Wise Hazel Tree just as I had imagined her~ strong and yielding!

And,

Mother Earth and Father Sky, the divine creators and protectors of all living things.

Author's Note

The story begins in the heartland with the tree-lined ravine of my childhood, at a time when the outdoors was my home away from home. The canopy of trees offered a seasonal backdrop to the day's play. My imagination, enchanted by the twisty roots of a tall elm tree, led me into hearty escapades with the forest inhabited creatures of olde world fables. I loved the seasons then, all of them, even winter. I forgot that for awhile, but I've remembered.

For me, writing rituals for seasonal living has as much to do with the innocent wisdom of make believe as it does the ancient teachings of elders. Make believe spins reality to our liking. To this day, I wish Thumbelina had been a childhood friend. I loved the earthy texture of her world. I wanted to sleep in the trees under a leaf woven coverlet, wear acorn hats at breakfast and flower petal dresses as I drifted lazily downstream in a walnut shell. I was intrigued with faerytales and other illustrated stories of fantasy brushed reality. I still am. And lest you're wondering, I'm brazenly sane. I've just always had this visceral interest in the unseen magick of the universe.

I've come to believe that living with the seasons reveals a magickal, panoramic view of our highest good. The unfolding of our true path cycles with the wheel of life just as nature does. By discovering the spiritual ebb and flow of seasons, we can adjust the timing of life and dreams to a more natural flow. Consider life's course if in autumn, we follow nature's cue and take stock of our accomplishments alongside harvest celebrations of nature's bounty. Or, as nature sleeps, we slow life's pace in winter to allow time for self-care and reflection. Once spring blooms, we would find ourselves more rested and ready to begin work on new ideas and ventures. Following our intention, the sunny days of summer would shine on our growing dreams and daily endeavors. Ultimately, living compatibly with the natural world not only sustains, but enlivens the planet and Her people.

One last thought, living seasonally reorients our sense of time to the present. It is within the present tense of life when synchronicity, the Great Mother's magickal elixir of right timing, person, place and thing is formulated. The resources necessary for life's challenges and dreams are brought to bear in the moment. I believe our true path is discovered by walking with nature and trusting in the Great Mother's ancient spiritual traditions as our guide. Reawakening the five senses to nature's gifts clears the way for the Great Mother to speak to us through the sixth sense, our intuition. She will not lead us astray.

Introduction

The Great Mother has been calling for humanity to live more compatibly with the natural world. The book is my contribution to the Mother's efforts to ensure the planet's survival and our spiritual unfolding, but with a slight twist. It's a call for action from a witch's perspective. Wicca, the olde religion of the Goddess honors the earth's divinity in ceremony and in living within the cycle of birth, death and rebirth. Paying attention to what is occurring outside in nature, and adjusting our internal barometer accordingly, helps us live more in season with the planet and manifest dreams more true to our divine human selves. The book gives readers, referred to as stewards, first hand ritual experience with the concept of living in season.

Rituals can facilitate the alignment of personal power with the natural forces at work. The book's twelve, monthly rituals are written with this outer/inner world attunement in mind. Stewards are guided on a spiritual, earth-centered odyssey to awaken the senses, all six of them. The design of the rituals reflects the author's Northern hemisphere and Midwest roots. Stewards who live elsewhere are encouraged to bring their own soil to the altar and adapt the rites as needed. The rituals may be performed alone or as part of a group. Besides a Wiccan orientation, the rituals are drawn from other ancient traditions including Astrology, Numerology and Feng Shui. In the book these traditions are symbolized as Branches of the Wise Hazel Tree. The Hazel tree is an ancient Celtic symbol of intuition inspired change and serves as a metaphor for the Crone, the elder phase of the Goddess in the book.

If these practices are unfamiliar, keep an open mind and don't worry. The appendix and glossary provide additional information on conducting a ritual and the book's use of the four ancient traditions. Also, the metaphysical seasoning is brewed with a measure of whimsy and nature's own ingredients making a delightfully sensual and spiritually rich ritual experience~ full bodied and nourishing for the soul. Awaiting us, after a spin around the wheel of life from whichever month the journey begins, is an invitation from the Great Mother to continue living life as a steward of Her soil and Our soul.

~ Blessed Be ~

All is Well in the Fall of the Leaves

Autumn~ A Time to:

Celebrate Accomplishments ~ September

Honor the Dead ~ October

Express Gratitude for the Bounty of Life ~ November

An Autumn Essay

We mark the seasons by the look of the trees, especially, in spring and autumn when they hold such an anticipatory place in our hearts. Annual road trips are planned to catch the turning of the leaves from summer to fall. Cresting a hill and beholding nature's canvas is divine. Earth's beauty catches the breath. The spectacular bluffs are nothing less than renderings of exquisite artistry. The brilliance of color burns into our senses casting our outlook in a golden blush. Radiant in their majesty, the trees stand tall, steadfast and content with their place in the world. Skyward bound, they accept our devotion and delight in the bewitching of the Mother's stewards.

Harvest celebrations follow the turn of the leaves. Fall is a time to observe the results of our labor to plant, nurture and manifest our dreams. The colors of autumn are the applause, the recognition of our individual accomplishments, in gloriously burnished, yellow, orange and red. Our own sweat and tears notwithstanding, the inspiration, expertise and encouragement received from our inner circle influences our ability to succeed. A humble heart recognizes the interdependent workings of success. With our dream in hand and our bounty now great, it is time to be grateful. In season we give thanks to those whose presence have enriched our lives.

The fall of the leaves is an outward showcase of the force of death, of letting go. Inherent in this cyclical demonstration of release, is a lesson for humanity on the benefit of setting free all that has served its purpose. Letting go and moving on is a natural result of a leaf, a life, a moment well lived. Sweeping the fallen leaves from our path ensures a surefooted journey. Each of us has experienced the exhilaration of finding ourselves on the other side of letting go. Once across, we feel our divinity pulsing with life, ready to reveal the next step on the path of our highest good.

This season make time to stand under the trees' autumn luster. Feel the soft caress of leaves as they drift to the ground. Listen to their wisdom in the howling wind. Watch as they scatter about spreading the message of fall. In this period of shorter days, indescribable color and ghostly hauntings, celebrate that which you have achieved. Honor the living and the dead for their unwavering support. Hold fast to what you have learned while letting go of all things no longer in keeping with your highest good. And, be grateful for life's bounty. All is Well in the Fall of the Leaves.

Chapter 1

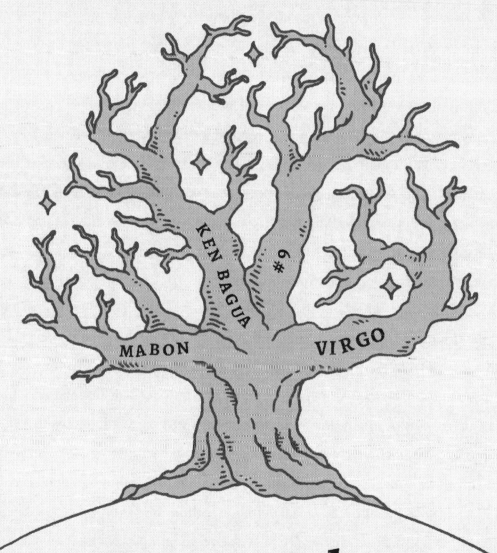

September

Celebrate Accomplishments

Carolann Gregoire, MSW

September's Sensual Nature

The first whiff of fall in early September fills our senses with all manner of things associated with school. Sometimes, the aromas are not always pleasant or appreciated. This could be because school signals the end of summer. Very few of us are ready to fall back into the daze of school. It's a shock to our collective system still accustomed to the carefree life of summer. We can empathize with parents and kids still in summer mode having to manage the frenzy of the first day back which arrives far too quickly. Like it or not though, there is nothing like the scent of school to ground a soul back in the pursuit of learning. The olfactory sense seems to work overtime inside educational walls. For grade-schoolers, pencil shavings and new crayons add to the new, shiny classroom smell. The power of the nose is not lost on parents. As we walk through the door we're hit with our own memories. The aroma of school disinfectant and floor polish conjures up our own set of recollections. For students, the taste of stadium hotdogs and brats will forever trigger the memory of infectious camaraderie and school spirit inspired by sporting events.

The sounds of school are also explicit, beginning with the change in street sounds from the flash of skateboard wheels to the lumbering groan of a school bus full of kids. The noise of classroom doors slamming shut, the click of shoes down the stairs and the hushed reprimands of students out in the hall flow in and out of earshot. The commonplace noise of school becomes embedded shaping to some degree how we will respond later to similar sounds. Hopefully, the more pleasant sensual offerings will outweigh the painful ones, such as the drumming of marching bands. Happening upon a practice after school is an unexpected treat. Whatever we were doing or thinking stops as the compelling beat pulls us into the moment. For a brief time our own internal rhythm is thrillingly in sync with something outside of ourselves. The musical pulsing of drums awakens the sleeping artist within and wishful thoughts of joining the band arise.

The weather is another influence on the feel of early September. The wind picks up blowing some of summer's heat away offering the crisp promise of cooler days to come. True to form, our day may begin with a morning walk in a hoodie and end with a stroll down to the coffee shop in flip flops. September is milder than August. But, the rains bring a damp mugginess to the air, reminding us that summer weather will continue to make appearances all the way to the end of the month. Fall storms in September are unlike October's. They thunder and bluster, but the leaves remain intact surviving green and lush. This quickens our appreciation of their protective canopy, soon to be gone.

The last of summer's garden also foretells the coming of fall. We pick the garden clean filling the Mother's cupboard one more time with fresh, ripe, juicy delights. Kitchen witches turn all manner of fruits and vegetables into frozen and canned edibles to be enjoyed during the winter months. Foods of September become more hearty and hot as the morning remains chilly after the night's cooling off. Savory recipes plucked from magazine pages become regular fall favorites. Kettles filled with onions and roots become tasty stews after a long days, slow simmer. Beverages served in ice-chilled glasses switch to earthen mugs filled hot to the brim.

And then there's the apple. Autumn is apple's turn to shine. The apple is a diverse fruit: some sweet, some tart, some better for cooking, some not. We partake of this fruit in all manner of ways: sliced, dipped, frittered, turned over and bobbed. This American staple is found in pies, cakes, salads and butter. Anyone fortunate to grow up with Granny Annie in the kitchen remembers this favorite orchard cobbler with crust made from scratch. Never wasting a scrap, leftover dough in granny's hands turns into squiggly, hot cinnamon crisps, simple but scrumptious. A slice of Granny Annie's apple spice and raisin nut cake drizzled with crème cheese frosting or served 'a la mode represents the hearth warming food sure to be found on September's table.

A Visit to the Wise Hazel Tree

The steward's belly is full with the fruits of September's bounty. Laying on his back, he looks up through the Wise Hazel Tree. The wind brushes leaves aside making it easier to see the intended branches. He counts four of them. The steward peers closer and sees that these particular branches are etched in the ancient languages of Astrology, Numerology, Feng Shui, and Wicca. Sensing his wonderment, the Tree tells the steward, "Settle yourself in, rest your back against my trunk and listen to the spirit of September's story written in the bark of the tree."

Branches of September's Wise Hazel Tree

Mabon~ Autumnal Equinox

Ken~ Knowledge & Spirituality Bagua

Vibration of 9

Sun in Virgo

The formal turning of the wheel to autumn occurs when the Sun crosses over the equator. The Sun's southern sojourn is known as the autumnal equinox. Those who love the Sun may grasp at summer's hot foothold all the way to the equinox at the end of the month. We who prefer fall tend to advance the wheel after the first crisp morning breeze. The Mother, understanding her children and their differences, indulges these seasonal liberties. The autumnal equinox is also known as Mabon and Harvest Moon. For farmers and witches alike, this day marks the point in time when dark and light are of equal length. An interesting side note is the discovery that the equinox date in both the Farmers and Wiccan Almanacs is the same. This may serve to allay the fears of those not as familiar with Wicca's earthen spiritual focus.

Followers of this olde religion are in tune with the changing season for similar reasons as those who work the land. In pagan lore, it is the passing of the reign of Lugh, the God of Light to his twin, Goronwy, the God of Dark. Under the rule of Goronwy, the light of day falls sooner under the night's veil. The growing season, in the absence of light, will come to an end. Mabon thus completes a bi-annual cycle. The vibration of the nine, September's number, propels the harvest towards completion, thus helping the Mother bring closure to this turn of the wheel. This phase of the harvest is only complete after we take stock of Her cupboard and conduct an inventory of the soul's growth.

As we harvest the bounty of the field so too we harvest the bounty of the soul. Ken, the I Ching's trigram representing the Knowledge and Spirituality Bagua, likens the harvesting of the soul to a time of quiet reflection and stillness. After a long day's toil, our inner recesses need space and time to gather and sift through experience to discern the significance of the journey. In stillness, the meaning rises to the surface as insight and knowledge gained. A courageous spirit is needed to seed and harvest a dream. Courage is needed further still to learn from dreams fulfilled and those not realized.

We turn to the Sun for help in this daring inventory of the soul. Under the influence of Mercury, the Sun in Virgo is persistent, almost relentless, in its drive toward accomplishment. The mental prowess of Virgo lends itself nicely to the state of mindfulness required this month. The Virgo rays cut like a knife lending precise, analytical energy to our endeavors. Virgo's practical quality can be a little too strident at times becoming perfectionist and overly critical of the self. To soften this exacting tendency, we call on the sign's earthy core to ensure a welcome inventory of our measure. To further prevent a misguided quest, Virgo's conscientious nature keeps a steady hand on our desires grounding them in earth-friendly pursuits.

We look to the bounty of the earth once more to retrieve a final tool to help harvest the soul. Buried deep within her belly lie the Mother's stones, her precious gems. Stones are in essence the result of Mother's alchemy of minerals, water, pressure and time. This magical mixture turns raw stones into tumbled tools under her spell. The versatile properties of stones serve many purposes beginning with their look and feel. We delight in the rainbow infused colors of Rubies, Emeralds and Topaz, the soft opaqueness of Moonstone and Opal, the bold lines of Malachite and the sparkly brush strokes of Peacock Ore. They bedazzle the eye and beg to be touched.

Another purpose of stones worthy of note is their powerful connection to ritual. A stone's influence can help harness our personal power to a particular intent by directing a focused beam of manifestation energy toward the goal. Therein lies the power of using Mother's jewels for magick and ritual. The Quartz Crystal is a beguiling example of the transformative power of stones. As a crystal pendant, it may grace a maiden's breast to release unrequited love. Hang it from a door frame in a multi-faceted cut to circulate chi as a Feng Shui cure, or the quartz may point to the future at the end of a pendulum's chain.

For use as a zodiac talisman this month, we pick Carnelian, a proud stone at once both warm and strong just like Virgo, the sign it complements. This commonly found stone is mined in radiant shades of orange ranging from light to the deep russet color of autumn. Not coincidentally, Carnelian's energetic properties are helpful in bringing clarity to a situation by heightening our awareness of the path upon which we are stepping. The spiritual beauty of the stone lies in its alliance with the earth. A cobblestone trail cut from autumn tinged Carnelian would surely entice a wayward wanderer back to the path, guiding and nurturing the soul once more.

Prepare for September's Ritual

If possible, perform the ritual at the Autumn Equinox.

~Seasonings for the Wise Hazel Tree's September Brew~

For the Ritual Altar~

An Altar Cloth

A Green Candle for the Divine

A Sun Gold Candle

A Scroll of Accomplishment

A Smudge Stick of Sage

A Bowl to Withstand the Fire's Flames

Stone of Carnelian for September's Intent

To Stand Next to a Symbol for Spirit

A Mother Earth Doll

Apple Spice Tea and Cornbread with Honey

And a Mix of Stones Scattered to Please

Nuggets from Nature Gathered While Out and About

Your Wand Made from a Stick

And, Last but Not Least, a Leaf Fallen from a Tree

Tasks Before the Ritual

1. Beginning with the first day of September~ Awaken with ears tuned to the sounds of the month. As you go about your morning, listen to September's voice inside and out~ no critiquing, just listening.

2. Take a walk or two or three. They need not be far, just long enough to delight your senses to September's look and feel and to gather up fallen nuggets from nature that please.

3. Make or embellish a Mother Earth doll in whatever fashion seems right.

4. Pack a lunch and set out on an apple harvest adventure. Picnic in the orchard and pick a bushel of September's fruit. In this season of giving, share your harvest with loved ones. And, if you're not too tired afterward, make something delicious from your

bounty~ a salad, a cobbler, or just bite into it and marvel at the look and taste of fruit picked, transported and prepared by you.

5.   Before the ritual may begin there are two final tasks that must be done first. Slip your Virgo stone of Carnelian into a pocket, and recite this meditation to aid you in this endeavor.

In stillness with the self and through quiet reflection

allow lessons learned to rise to the surface.

Ponder the wisdom gained through lessons and deeds

especially those you toiled so hard to achieve.

Now narrow the list to include those of late~ the goals

you nurtured since last September's date.

Select when ready~ those worthy of note,

then, pen them to paper.

We'll celebrate later.

Secondly, make your list into a scroll using ribbon to

tie~ storing it someplace safe and nearby.

6.   Select a charm that symbolizes the insight gained from your accomplishments and attach it to the wand.

<u>The Day of the Ritual</u>

Prepare the Ritual Feast~

Brew your apple spice tea with charged water. Homemade or not, cornbread

with honey is a scrumptious complement to our fall flavored drink.

Placement of the Altar~

Lay the altar cloth on the table

For the four directions~

Wand and the burning bowl with sage in the East

Sun Gold candle in the South

Moon refreshments in the West

Nuggets and leaf in the North

Place the green candle in the center to represent the divine

Lay the Carnelian stone and symbol for spirit before the candle

Set the Mother Earth doll near the center

Place the Scroll of Accomplishment next to the Sun's candle

Cover the altar with stones made from the earth, scattering them about for Mother's mirth.

Now add what you please, make it your own, with a touch of whimsy the altar transforms.

Time to Center and Smudge~

Cast the Circle~

Invite the Directions~

Reader:

Welcome Direction of East, Spirit of Wind. Feel the crisp brush of air upon

your cheek while you listen to autumn's muse. The dream inspired melody is

carried on the wind and sung in soulful notes by the morning dove. In harmony

they sing keeping time and beat with the jittery hum of the cicada.

Our mind now clear wiped fresh by the wind is ready to receive this choral blessing.

Welcome Direction of South, Spirit of Flame. With an intake of breath,

draw in the stove's wood tinged smoke. With autumn filled chest

breathe out summer's ashes, the last of the campfire's embers.

Now light the Sun's candle~ match to flame~ dreams to achievement.

Welcome Direction of West, Spirit of Heart. Be mindful as you eat and

drink from Her cupboard the last of Mother's crop. Each mouthful as sweet

as the gratitude we feel as our hearts swell as big as our tummies.

When full, offer thanks to the Mother and loved ones for their support of our dreams.

(Enjoy the Mother's treats.)

Welcome Direction of North, Spirit of Earth. Behold in reverence nature's

nuggets and leaf. Picked for protection from our human misdeeds.

Honored in ritual, nature's treasures are symbols for living compatibly with thee.

Welcome Mother Earth and Father Sky. We are blessed

by your presence at September's table.

We are your stewards. As you sustain us so shall we sustain the earth.

Light the green candle to turn the flame divine.

An Autumn Tale

A Walk in the Field

With Sage Doe Walker

Reader:

The doe noticed the bright afternoon Sun slipping sooner into dusk. She paused long enough to breathe in the orange waves of sunset. Then, continued her slow ambling pace through the harvest turned field. She stopped to sniff the earth. The faint smell of wheat hung in the upturned soil. She gently chewed the few remaining straws poking up from beneath.

It had been a busy growing season. She had a lot to sort through in her mind. To help clear the unimportant from the important, the doe moved as if in a ritual~ walking a few steps, stopping to turn the soil, eating the remnants of harvest. It was relaxing. Her body took over to let her mind wander. Untethered, her thoughts skipped from one thing to another. The doe didn't mind. She noted the thoughts and sent them on their way. Slowly, little by little, clarity took form and the image she was waiting for appeared to her.

Sage Doe Walker stood still, ears twitching, heart fluttering as the male figure walked toward her. Once alongside, he took measure of how much she had grown since last season. He was clearly delighted with his assessment. She stood proud, wiggling a bit as he scratched behind her ears.

They stood together, the doe and God Lugh, quietly surveying the field. Lugh took a deep breath filling his lungs with the fresh harvest scent and remarked, "I don't know which I like best, the first breath of a dewy spring morn or this, autumn's twilight musk. Not that it matters. I will miss it all especially, the Sun." The doe nuzzled his chest in comfort.

After more moments of quiet, Lugh turned to Sage and asked," Do tell little one how did the season treat you?" "Very well, I believe." "I think I figured out how I can best serve the Mother." God Lugh chuckled and said, "That certainly sounds like a grand achievement!" "I don't mean it to sound boastful, Sage Doe Walker shyly replied. In fact, I think what I learned is that serving Her doesn't have to be big."

"I spent a lot of time in this field, watching it grow, being careful not to eat too much. I looked where I stepped and worried with the steward when the rains didn't come and then came too much. I talked to the Mother every day. After about the umpteenth time I asked her how I could help," She told me," to stop fretting and keep doing what I was doing." "The Mother wouldn't tell me what that was exactly."

"I'm trying not to worry so much and actually have more days than not when I don't. On the good days I seem to make my way easier and feel more connected to Her. I see things better and find little ways to be helpful. After one of the good days, I rest easier at night and have happier dreams. It's hard not to worry though." "Yes, it is little doe," said Lugh. "So, when you're having a fretful day, what helps?" Sage Doe Walker replied, "I say this to myself over and over until it takes."

This day is mine to make.

Painted with chosen colors of the past,

on canvas faintly etched in tomorrow.

God Lugh moved closer to Sage Doe Walker and put his arm across her back. Together, they watched as the Harvest Moon made her ascent in the night sky. God Lugh took one last breath of his reign and sighed contentedly. As he exhaled he quietly affirmed, "This night is mine to make. Painted with chosen colors of the past, on canvas faintly etched in tomorrow."

Celebration Incantation

Led by God Lugh

Reader, instruct the stewards to hold their stones of Carnelian or put them in their pockets as you recite as God Lugh:

One lone tree turns, green on the bottom, russet on top

mirroring September's journey.

Toil to Insight~ Green to Russet.

Reader, instruct the stewards to hold their scrolls next to their hearts as they:

Breathe in green the color of abundance,

breathe in again~ the color of insight, autumn's russet.

Reader, instruct the stewards to hold their Scrolls of Accomplishments near the green candle's flame and resume as God Lugh:

Dream to seed, seed to bloom,

bloom to bounty,

wisdom gained.

Reader, invite each steward to unfurl their Scroll of Accomplishments one by one and recite:

Great Mother Earth and Gods of Light and Dark,

by your power and my deeds, I celebrate these accomplishments in ritual with thee.

Reader, invite the stewards to read from their Scrolls of Accomplishments silently or out loud

Reader, once done, Exclaim:

Gods and Goddesses of Mabon, Spirits of the Four Corners,

join with me in Blessing and Merriment

our toil to insight is now complete.

Now wise and content we journey forward.

Choosing a path made clear by Mother's Carnelian,

we step into the future on the soles of the Steward.

The Turn to Mabon

Reader:

Lugh, God of Light, sunshine of the growing season our

bounty is great through your divine grace.

Our arms are full with harvest grain.

Our hearts once weary are now sustained.

Light and Dark standing side by side~ Advance the wheel forward while equal in power.

Goronwy, God of Dark, moonshine of the sleeping season your rise has come.

In stillness and cover of night we turn within for rest and

renewal~ protected and safe in your keep.

Open the Circle~

You may open the circle after you have finished your tea and treat and offer

thanks to our guests for their presence and protection at September's table ~

Mother Earth

Gods Lugh & Goronwy

the 4 Directions

& Sage Doe Walker

<u>After the Ritual</u>

The accomplishments framed or left as a scroll remain as a symbol for

dreams yet to be. Place the symbol in the Fame & Reputation Bagua for

future manifestation. Achievements of past placed in this Bagua ignite

ember into flame~ kindling for life's kiln~ fuel for our dreams.

A daily affirmation to propel you forward into the future may be said throughout the

rest of September in the Knowledge & Spirituality Bagua of the home or room.

Light the green candle and recite:

My toil to insight is now complete.

Wise and content I journey forward.

Choosing a path made clear by Mother's Carnelian,

I step into my future on the soles of the Steward.

On the last day of the month you may keep the Carnelian stone in the Knowledge &

Spirituality Bagua as a symbol for living in season with the month of September.

All is Well in the Fall of the Leaves

~ Blessed Be ~

Chapter 2

October

Honor the Dead

Carolann Gregoire, MSW

October's Sensual Nature

The scents and flavors of autumn's second month are heady and strong. Outside, there is a somewhat pleasant, sweet, pungent smell to the earth as plants and leaves begin to decay. Inside, candles, potpourri and foods are infused with the unmistakable herbs of fall. Nutmeg, clove and cinnamon- laced delectables fire up the appetite making the treats irresistible especially, when served with a dollop of whipped cream. Whipped cream, the topping of the Goddess, delights the body and soul when plopped and squirted atop coffee drinks, toddies and pumpkin pie. Apples continue to be a featured fruit when drank as cider or eaten with a nut dusted caramel coating. About the only time we aren't glad to see an apple is if it shows up in a trick-or-treat bag.

After the equinox, the vestiges of summer mingle a bit with early October before fall takes over. Days continue to warm up, but nights cool off requiring layers of clothes buttoned up in the morning to be peeled off mid-day and zipped up again before bedtime. After awhile, nature's beauty changes venue from a summer landscape to the gallery of the trees. Bits of trees turn yellow and red just enough to herald the advent of autumn. Knowing the rapture is short-lived, the first brazen color always leaves a bittersweet awareness in the heart. For as gorgeous as fall is, it stands between summer, the season most savored and winter, the season many anticipate with a sense of foreboding.

Thankfully, we are spellbound each day by the magical allure of October. The Sun bouncing off the golden, scarlet and deep purple leaves casts October in a crystal amber glow. Even when raining, the look of the day is bathed in rich, earthy tones. When the leaves begin to fall, streets become leaf splattered asphalt, a black canvas to showcase the autumn palette. Leaves underfoot rustle and crunch as we snake our way down wooded trails. Falling acorns add to the musical composition as they plink and plunk their way from branches to rooftops, to car hoods and pavement. We allow ourselves to embrace homespun traditions this time of the year and enjoy hayrides, barn dances and s'mores by the fire. Hopefully, you are old enough to remember the smell of burning leaves and experience the cozy comfort the memory conjures.

Evening is eerie time in October. Tis the time when hauntings occur. Imagined or real there is no getting around the otherworldly feel of autumn's spooky month. It is unnerving for a reason. The falling of the leaves signals the death of the growing cycle for all of nature. Just as late October storms come along to shake off the leaves still hanging on, we too need a shake up at times to let go, release the old, the past and what we no longer need. Rebirth is smoother, easier, more straightforward if new buds, seeds of ideas are unencumbered by stuck, stiff and mildewed specks of life. Mother Nature, recognizing our challenge with letting go, brings closure to the growing cycle and harvest season through the brilliance of color. Autumn's magick captivates and mesmerizes, helping us accept this literal and figurative death.

A Visit to the Wise Hazel Tree

The blustery weather sends a shiver down the steward's spine as he watches the wind shake the Wise Hazel Tree half bare. He instinctively inches closer to Her for protection and knocks his head on a branch. His impulse to lash out is curbed by the markings he notes on the bark. The ancient traditions carved into the Tree are now more visible. He peers closer until another shiver sends him looking here and there for the unseen made seen this night. The Tree warns the steward to, "Get comfortable, zip up your jacket! And, above all else keep your eyes peeled as the Crone tells the tale of All Hallow's Eve."

Branches of October's Wise Hazel Tree

Samhain~ All Hallow's Eve~ Halloween

Ch'ien~ Helpful People & Travel Bagua

Vibration of 1

Sun in Libra

Before we begin the tale of All Hallow's Eve, we have a

little matter to clear up about the witch~

Believe not in the hooded figure of the hag. Tis better to look upon her as the wise,

old Crone. For truth be told, before she was defamed by the new religion, the ancient

Crone was revered for her wisdom and power nurtured under the Wise Hazel Tree.

The former image of the Crone sustained since the burning times makes her impossible not to revile and fear. This historical dismantling of the Crone's respect and power may contribute today to the persistent devaluing of our elders and their cultural contribution. In Wiccan tradition, the Crone is valued as the elder phase of the Moon, the senior chapter in the life of the triple Goddess. After serving the Great Mother as maiden and mother, the Crone reigns in an exalted position reached through the wisdom of experience shared with the world.

Notwithstanding the myth of the Crone as an 'old hag', modern Halloween highly resembles one of the pagan holy days, Samhain, also referred to as All Hallow's Eve. For the ancient Celts, it was a celebratory night of completion. Samhain honors the last of the harvest months, the last day of the pagan year, and the death of the Sun God, Yule. The revelry had a somber note due to the significance of these transitions. But, true to pagan sensibility, merriment prevailed during the feast. After all, there was bounty to enjoy and matters to put to rest. The merriment and the belief in the rebirth of the God at the winter solstice all served to uplift a heavy heart.

Death and hauntings figure prominently in both the old and new holiday however, these elements are approached differently between the traditions. They are the most riveting aspects unifying contemporary Halloween with the pagan, All Hallow's Eve. As the olde story is told, it is the night in which the veil separating the worlds of the living and the dead is most transparent. The living and the dead may enjoy a closer proximity to one another. Spirits may cross through the veil visiting their old haunts and living ancestors. It is this very point in the story where the old spooky lore gets twisted into an evil tinged night of ghouls.

As the old pagan ways became perceptually more threatening to the new world order, a vile, breech of moral conduct under the guise of religious cleansing occurred. Stories equating the followers of the Goddess with evil, even satanic forces were spread creating a religious holocaust eventually, forever tarnishing the image of the witch and her true purpose. Edain McCoy discusses the damaged image of the witch in his book, *Sabbats*. Her cauldron and broomstick, symbols of the union between the divine feminine and masculine, became instruments associated with dark magic and harassment. Gradually as the pagan way of life waned, the witch as Crone became the distorted hag and the holiday's embodiment of evil. The notion of a familiar, a willing four legged companion of light magic became the black cat. Our familiar and pet was now a skulking fearsome feline best never to cross.

Pumpkins and jack-o-lanterns even figured into the deception. This gourd exemplified the strategy of switching the face of light magic to dark. During All Hallow's Eve, the night before the New Year, pagans desiring a visit from spirits would place a lit candle in the window to guide the spirit home. Sometimes, harvest gourds carved in welcome served the same purpose. Scary faces were engraved on some pumpkins to protect the pagans from unwanted visits from lost or less than benevolent spirits. As the reputation of the Celtic New Year's Eve became a more sinister night to fear and less a communion with welcomed spirits, the face of the jack-o-lantern became more ominous. The menacing sneers served as protection from not only wayward spirits, but spirits in general. Visitation from the dead was cast in a frightful light becoming a decidedly unwelcome sight.

In this lifetime, contemporary Halloween has withstood an imposed gauntlet. For a brief period of time, the holiday was banned in some schools and communities for its supposed satanic roots. The fear of succumbing to evil's seduction is a dark current that runs through the religious faithful. Witnessing the resurgence of Halloween's tarnished image is not surprising during times of heightened religious fervor. Faceless evil is too much to bear. Throughout history, those most different from ourselves, especially in matters of religion, fall prey to the face of evil. Thankfully, this time the banning was short-lived and without physical malice. Today, we are free to enjoy its beloved status as a fiendishly friendly holiday whose decoration almost rivals that of Christmas. Warts and all, Halloween today serves as a reminder of the old ways and a living symbol of the sustaining power of the Crone.

October's ritual honors the Sabbat of Samhain restoring its true purpose with due respect and reverence. Before and during the ritual we will invite spirits of ancestors and mentors in celebration of their influence upon our lives. The process of letting go will be literally and figuratively evident in the sensual and spiritual aspects of the month. October's altar will be scattered with bits of fallen nature in recognition of this necessary cycle of life. Prior to the ritual, our hallowed work of the month will enable the release of unwanted memories, patterns and relationships no longer serving our highest good. Rebirth follows death and so, death is not to be feared.

We first call upon the ancient tradition of Feng Shui to help us complete the business of the ritual: we must sweep the cobwebs out of our heart and welcome travelers from the other side. As unlikely as it sounds, the Helpful People and Travel Bagua is the most spiritually potent. According to the I Ching trigram, Ch'ien is where our spiritual leaders and icons rest most comfortably. In a broader sense, helpful people are also our ancestors and mentors both living and dead. This Bagua honors their inspiration, comfort and support. One of the tasks completed prior to the ritual uses this Bagua to set the tone for welcoming the desired spirits to the sacred circle. If possible, use this space to conduct the hallowed work of the month. Surrounding the steward in spiritual grace will make for a more ease-filled release. Reciting the daily affirmations in the chosen space will further direct the Bagua's energy to help us manage any residual tension from discarding unwanted habits.

Venus is known for breathing a spark of lively, festive fun into social gatherings as is another spiritual guest, Lord Misrule. Venus, the Roman Goddess of Love and beauty is the ruler of Libra, our Sun kissed sign of the month. We call upon her to save the ritual from becoming overly grave and gloomy by casting the night in sensual ambience. Lord Misrule enjoys a spirited reputation for mischievous merriment. His antics help to distract us from the holiday's heavy emotional undertone. Bewitched by their loving and joyful presence, October's multi-dimensional night of revelry should be grand in scale and alternately amusing, serious and spooky.

Libra compliments the merry and somber elements of the month's intention quite well. Sometimes, Libra's love of beauty and gracious ways can be mistaken for superficiality. In fairness, this genteel side of Libra balances the sign's charge of securing justice and equality in matters of life. Balancing the scales in equal measure is a weighty and heavy responsibility. This is a duty made achievable with the help of Venus. A loving touch during introspective and life appraising times, can tip the scales toward a future with promise rather than remaining stuck in an unfulfilling past.

A balanced and whole life requires cycles of death and rebirth. If we are to move forward on the path of our highest good we must release that which is no longer in keeping with our sacred journey. With Venus and Periodot, Libra's companion stone, by our side we can lovingly and decisively release the stuck, stiff and mildewed specks of life keeping us from our true self and path. Adorned at the throat, Periodot helps the steward clear the muck hiding our intuition from view. The discarding of old baggage allows for our intuition to guide us more directly towards the next journey, rebirth. Once our hallowed work is done, the pioneering vibration of number one rises to the surface and kicks off the Celtic New Year to a grand start~ Cheers to our new adventures.

Prepare for October's Ritual

If possible, perform the ritual at All Hallow's Eve.

~ Seasonings for the Wise Hazel Tree's October Brew ~

For the Ritual Altar~

An Altar Cloth

Black and Lime Green Witch Candles

A Smudge Stick of Sage

and a Skeleton Key

A Cauldron with a Black Votive set in her Belly

A Broomstick to Keep Spooky Spirits at Bay

A Hallowed Writ of Stuck, Stiff and Mildewed Specks of Life

Stone of Peridot, Symbol of October's Intent

To Stand Near a Symbol for Spirit

Acorns and Leaves Gathered While Out and About

A Friendly Face Jack-o-Lantern

A Crone Doll

A Divination Tool

Irish Breakfast Tea brewed with charged water and Lemon

Served with a Slice of Pumpkin Pie and a Dollop of Whipped Cream

And, Last but Not Least, the Stick Turned into a Wand

Tasks Before the Ritual

1. Make or buy a broomstick. A shop selling crafts and seasonal goods is a likely spot to find one. Place beside the fireplace or front door to protect the home from negative energy.

2. Fashion a Crone doll or use a favorite Crone Halloween decoration.

2. Gather acorns and leaves while taking your walks to decorate the altar most seasonally.

3. Gather pumpkins this year from a farmer's or community run market, better yet make a day of it with loved ones and harvest at least two from a nearby pumpkin patch~

one for the altar and one for trick-or-treat. Place both pumpkins in the Helpful People & Travel Bagua to soak the harvest gourds in the spiritual energy.

4. The night before the ritual, carve a friendly face on the altar jack-o-lantern. While creating a face of welcome, bring to heart and mind the spirits you wish to invite to the ritual.

5. When time, carve the trick-or-treat pumpkin to tickle and please.

6. String a single bead of Periodot with silver or cord to fashion a hallowed necklace.

7. When ready, place the hallowed necklace around your neck and begin the work of release and letting go. Recite this meditation for guidance.

Any baggage is fair game.

The only rule is that you're ready and willing to burn it in flame.

Forgiveness of self and others is at play,

stay above the pull to shame and blame.

Once the baggage is named,

record it on paper for release in the fire.

For specks of life not ready for toss,

be gentle with the self for all is not lost.

Place the rest in the hands of your guides,

who'll watch over the specks

without taking sides

until, tossed onto coals, flecks onto fire.

Make a Hallowed writ by writing down those specks of life you are willing to release.

8. And, last but not least the charm for the wand. Choose from October's intent a symbol of death either to honor the spirits or your work of release made sacred the night of All Hallow's Eve.

The Day of the Ritual

Prepare the Feast~

Use your charged water to brew your Moon kissed Irish Breakfast tea. Homemade pumpkin pie is delicious but, store bought slathered in whipped cream is a county fair's second best.

Placement of the Altar~

Lay the altar cloth on the table

For the four directions~

Wand, sage, and key in the East

Black votive in the cauldron's belly for the South

Mother's treats in the West

Acorns and leaves in the North

Place the black and green candles in the center to represent

the Crone and her God in his passing

Lay the symbol for spirit before the candles

Stand the Crone doll next to the symbol for spirit

Lay the Hallowed Writ and Periodot necklace beside the cauldron

Put the divination tool in front of the candles to absorb divine wisdom

When not in use stand the broomstick within the sacred circle

facing East to protect the festivities from uninvited guests

Center the jack-o-lantern amongst the Mother's acorns and leaves to

help ground the spirits within the sacred circle upon their arrival

Now add your own touch making the space as spooky as you please

Time to Center and Smudge ~

Before you perform the centering and smudging, take the witch's

broom and sweep the negative energy out of the ritual space.

Cast the Circle ~

Invite the Directions ~

Reader:

Welcome Direction of East, Spirit of the Unseen. Brush the cobwebs from the

brow~ the sleep from the eye. Open the door to the interior~ where intuition, the

otherworldly sense resides~ behold what's ahead, the vision unveiled this nite.

Welcome Direction of South, Spirit of Death and Rebirth. (Light the candle inside the cauldron.) The leaves once brazen from the Sun lie curled and dry upon the earth. Their day is done, their life now spent, the cycle of life and death complete. Toss the leaves crushed by hand into the cauldron's flame. Offer thanks to the Crone as they stage one last show in brilliant fire.

Welcome Direction of West, Spirit of the Hearth. A balance must be struck between this nite's somber yet merry truth. Presiding over the festivities in matching royal purple and sitting atop velvet lined scales are Venus, Goddess of Love and her consort, the mischievous Lord of Misrule. They decree in unison, "Stewards of the Mother~ October's feast is ready. As our guests, please~ eat, drink and be merry."

Welcome Direction of North, Touchstone Spirit of Earth. Centered with the Mother, soul tethered to the ground~ off we go for a spin on the broom, riding into the night for a flight to the stars and a dance on the Moon.

Welcome Mother Earth and Father Sky. Light the black and green candles as you recite, a final look back on the eve of the New Year reveals divine footprints visible next to those of the stewards. Always by our side we have been blessed by your presence yesterday~ and today, as we turn the wheel together at October's table.

Jack-O-Lantern Incantation

Reader, recite as Lord Misrule:

Ghosts, Ghouls, and Goblins~ spirit names of the dead,
I hold the key unlocking the door between my world and yours.
Enter once invited, leave on my command.
Our circle is open if this rule is obeyed~ you must play nice!
Show any fiendish displays and the door will appear
snatching you back from whence you came.
Now go,
mingle, make merry and say what you need.
At the close of the eve you will take your leave.

Reader, light the jack-o-lantern sitting in the North corner. Instruct the stewards to go around the circle, each having an opportunity if so desired to invite spirits of loved ones and mentors. Light your personal jack-o-lantern to welcome them to the table.

Out of the Ashes~ A Crone's Tale

An All Hallow's Eve Reading

Reader, recite as the Crone:

Once upon a time, the healer in the woods brought life to the world, made love with abandon, kissed tears of woe and helped spirits pass through the door.

A life made simple by heeding Mother's cue, the Crone lived in season. Breathing in joy and pain, these gifts of the day made her strong and wise.

Wrapped in a cloak spun from the spider's silk she walked the hills offering solace and healing to the Mother's stewards until~ the day the sky burned red. Some witches survived, others did not. All were innocent in the Court of Divine Law.

For years, too many to recall~ the followers of the Goddess practiced witchcraft in darkness. Everyday items used as implements of magick worked for awhile. But, eventually even her broomstick and cauldron were mistook for utensils of evil.

The Religion of the Goddess, though reduced in stature, was never abolished to the bane of the new world's order. The spirit of the Great Mother lived on and was passed from generation to generation from the tales of the Crone told to the mother and the maiden.

Be ye a steward wrapped in spider spun cloak or some other weave~ we can honor and play together this nite costumed in mantles of green~ and witness the Wheel of Life turn once more toward the Mother.

Our tale ends as it once began. Risen from the ashes, the healer in the woods brings life to the world, kisses tears of woe, makes love with abandon~ And this nite as before~ helps spirits pass through the door.

Spell to Release Stuck, Stiff, and Mildewed Specks of Life

Reader, instruct the stewards to hang the necklace of Periodot around their neck and hold the Hallowed Writ near the Cauldron's Flame. Going around the circle each steward may read silently or out loud from their Hallowed Writ and release their Specks of Life into the Cauldron's flame. After the Hallowed Writs have been cast into the cauldron, recite this spell:

A life, a leaf, a moment lived,

lessons to learn,

experience to heed.

My body full with specks of life,

If helpful still~ you may remain.

If not, with a respectful tug I set you free!

Harder to release are the specks~ stuck, stiff, and mildewed with age.

These require a harder pull from hands entwined with Divine Grace.

Together we pluck those specks loosened up.

The rest I place in the hands of Grace

until the day, with a respectful tug I set them free!

Divination Incantation

Reader:

Safe and protected within the sacred circle,

the door to the interior world opens wide,

where intuitive discourse comes to mind.

This is a nite of finality~ the cycle of life and death comes to an end.

Sorrow but a little, rebirth is the beginning,

a promise of the Mother

made easier now that specks of life have been released.

Seek not too far into the future.

Tomorrow unfolds starting today.

Rather, ask this question to help the Wheel Turn~

What do I need to hear this nite to help my rebirth at Yule?

Mother Earth, Father Sky, Goddess Venus, Lord of Misrule,

Spirits of the Four Corners and other invited guests,

my otherworldly sense is open to receive your wisdom and blessing.

Thank you and Blessed Be!

Reader: Stewards, you may now proceed with the Divination Tool of choice. Do not be surprised if messages are relayed throughout the celebration and even into your nighttime dreams.

Feel free to include other spells, the month of October is ripe for magick.

Open the Circle ~

When the magick making and feast is complete you may open the circle after offering thanks to our divine spirits for their protection and help this evening ~

The Crone, and her God

Goddess Venus

Lord of Misrule

Ghosts, Ghouls and Goblins

Her Familiar

and Other Invited Spirits

And, after releasing the spirits from whence they came~

Reader, recite as Goddess Venus:

Ghosts, Ghouls, Goblins

and Other Invited Spirits,

our bodies now spent from the nite's merriment

are full from the feast and communion with thee.

The veil between worlds transparent this eve

darkens as the door shuts, locked with the key.

Shed No Tears, Cry Not in Fear,

the veil is crafted in spellbound weave

with threads blessed by your essence,

watched over with care by your loved ones and me.

Reader, instruct the stewards to blow out their jack-o-lantern.

After the Ritual~ an Affirmation

The day after the ritual place your symbol for spirit, the jack-o-lantern, Hallowed necklace, and a witch candle in the Helpful People & Travel Bagua of the home or room. Light the candle and place the necklace around your neck while you recite this affirmation~

A life, a leaf, a moment lived,

lessons to learn,

experience to heed.

My body full with specks of life,

if helpful still~ you may remain.

If not, with a respectful tug I set you free!

This affirmation helps prevent the released specks of life from returning and manage any residual tension from the experience. You may leave the Hallowed necklace in the space as a reminder of October's Grace.

All is Well in the Fall of the Leaves

~ Blessed Be ~

Chapter 3

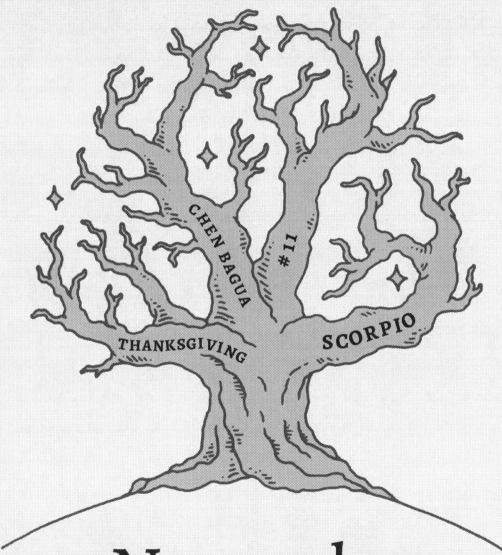

CHEN BAGUA

#11

THANKSGIVING

SCORPIO

November

Express Gratitude for Life's Bounty

November's Sensual Nature

Resting, so to speak between two festive months, November sometimes struggles with its own identity. Mannequins in shop windows are stripped of their warm autumn woolens and replaced with winter robed Saint Nicks long before Halloween has come and gone. Depending upon the weather, the month can feel more like winter but, the wheel doesn't officially turn until late December. It's the Mother's curtain call, the last show of the season. If not for Thanksgiving, we might miss the subtle offerings of the month. Whereas, October is warm enough to keep us busy with outside activities, November's chilly gray days begin the cycle of turning within.

In autumn's final landscape, we watch with a downward eye as the land sheds its crush of color. Trees still scarlet and gold are viewed through the naked lens of their barren brothers. The glow of autumn turns underfoot. After a rain, the lamplight dancing off wet fallen leaves lights a walk at dusk in sparkling amber. The early morning haze hovering just above the brown and golden groundcover foretells the coming frost. After, hearty mums begin to curl inward but somehow retain their bushy pose to the last. For those not wary of winter, November is a wickedly destructive month. Mother nature whips, spins and turns around upending bits of nature in her path. Her whirlwind becomes frenzied pulling leaves from branches and knocking dead limbs from trees. All that is done in this life comes falling down.

By the end of the month, only the sturdiest of the green remains. The rest either sleeps or is foraged for winter. Squirrels sniff and taste every last nut for their nutritional endurance over the cold months ahead. They are a busy little creature representing nature's sensual purpose of making ready for winter. Only that which is vitally necessary for sustenance and rebirth in the spring is maintained. Nests, hovels, dams and burrows are fortified with leaves, twigs, bits of string and other discarded human trappings. All is stripped clean right down to the bare essence of survival.

Humans make ready for winter as well. We winterize our homes, cars and bodies. Closets are switched out from summer wear to cold weather clothes. Furnace filters are changed. Tires are checked and rotated. We top off wiper fluid and anti-freeze all in anticipation of the upcoming season. These and other November activities are the modern analogs of what our ancestors must have done in preparation for surviving the long winter nights. It is no wonder that the quieting magic of November is lost when we are so consumed with what is coming next.

Thankfully, we do remember to honor the last of the season's bounty, the cornucopia of squash, pumpkins and gourds picked from muted rows of eggplant, ocher and sage colored vegetables. How can we not appreciate the last of the welcoming, earthy harvest of plenty? Especially, when adding coconut, clove and brown sugar, the nuts and spices of fall, to November's harvest table. We place about our homes, bowls filled with shelled and unshelled peanuts, salty and honey roasted cashews, trail mix and other exotic and assorted nuts to fatten us up for winter. Many of our recipes this month include pecans, walnuts and shaved coconut such as Dad's Salad, a fruity concoction that calls for cups of this and that. Americans love their starch and turn to comfort foods once the cold hits, like our favored root of the month, the sweet potato. You can do just about anything to this root and we will eat it: bake it plain, fry it up, or whip and top it with marshmallows and nuts. Or, you can wait until after Thanksgiving dinner and spoon in mouthfuls of sweet potato pie.

It is the time of the year when we express our gratitude for life's bounty at the annual gathering of family and friends around a thankful hearth. For one glorious holiday we relish, savor and remember a time when lard, mother's staple was appreciated for its hygienic and cooking value. It is one of two times of the year when we allow ourselves to enjoy food in all its rich, buttery, ancestral glory. We indulge and indulge again later that night and into the next day in scrumptious dishes and leftovers. It's also during this holiday of gratefulness when we measure our cup of life full. Individuals, families and communities rise to the occasion overcoming for one day our propensity to ruminate on the dark, fearful and unsatisfied moments of life. As individuals and as a nation of people, our challenge is to envision a plentiful life connected as one, entwined with all that is. This is the gift and quest of November.

A Visit to the Wise Hazel Tree

Once the winds finally cease, the Wise Hazel Tree raises her branches. Tired and a little shaken, she looks out across autumn's landscape. The Tree is content with the look of her land~ satisfied with the plentiful bounty ~ sure in the knowledge her branches impart. Feeling his cold through the branches protecting him from the storm, the Tree wraps a woolen scarf around the neck of the steward and draws him closer. Warm and comfortable, he rests against her sturdy trunk and watches for November's story viewed through the barren lens of the trees.

Branches of November's Wise Hazel Tree

A Day of Thanksgiving

Chen~ Health & Family Bagua

Vibration of 11

Sun in Scorpio

A life of plenty should not be mistaken for a life of greed. An abundant heart feeds the soul and the souls of others. Contentment is a soft rippling feeling of being and having enough. Although each of us defines the measure of enough and the ingredients differently, the resulting sigh of contentment is universal. As a people, we face two challenges with abundance. First, we must secure personal fulfillment without defining ourselves and others as selfish. Then, our call is to help others do the same.

Failure to nurture ourselves and others results in lives half filled allowing misery to seep into the empty space. Lack and overindulgence can result in similar emotional predicaments: fear of not having what we need and want or, fear of losing what we have achieved. Unchecked fear breeds discontent and despair. It can lead to grasping on too tight, hoarding what we have. In this polarized challenge, the individual has generally given others the power to make or break life. We either wait for someone to fill us up or wait for someone to take it away.

The irony of abundance is that when a cup is full enough from our personal effort and perhaps, some help from others, it wants to spill over into another's cup. Filling up and spilling over is a natural balancing mechanism of the Mother. It not only helps others achieve, but also keeps the contents of our cup fresh and true to our evolving path. If there is no other cup to catch the overflow, abundance becomes merely self serving. Worse yet, it may actually disrupt the natural ebb and flow of a plentiful existence, eventually drying up our cup, our life. What we give to the world or not will come back to us in kind. One for all and all for one keeps the Mother's wellspring of abundance flowing.

The natural order of life rests in our connection to one another and all that is. As earth bound spirits, we are neither dependent or independent by nature. Interdependence is a better concept to describe our relationship with others, the planet and the universal spirit. An enlightened path crisscrosses with other beings from here and the other side consciously and in altered states. In an ideal world we would sense the unbreakable thread joining us together. We would seek that which fulfills without wasting, stealing, or hoarding from others. Personal responsibility would be the norm, defined in this context as the ability to wield power wisely and judiciously. Securing just enough abundance and sharing the rest in a small or grand scale with the rest of the planet is our task.

We can live a life of plenty by following the natural world's lead. Fall is an opportune time in which to begin. In September, we celebrated personal accomplishments and nature's harvest. We recognized the contributions of others in our achievements. In October, we honored deceased spirits. We let go of unnecessary specks of life just as nature shed blooms and leaves to ensure enough nourishment for the roots until spring. This month, we take our cue from the squirrels as they store nuts for the winter. We ready ourselves for the coming quiet time by storing blessings in our now spacious heart, by expressing gratitude for the universal bounty of life. Our journey requires a willingness to begin settling into the darkness, to go within and trace the thread of individual and collective bounty back to the universal root of the Great Mother.

Gratefulness in its own right is a valuable life lesson as it teaches us to recognize the impact of others upon our existence. Abundance also manifests more fluidly through a grateful heart. A state of grace is the expanded spiritual awareness of the energetic relationship between personal, communal and universal abundance. Therefore, rather than being a month cast in the shadows by the rest of autumn, November is actually a rather spiritually intense time of the year. The quest beckons us to envision a plentiful life, connected as one and entwined with all that is.

Thankfully, the ancient traditions for November coincide precisely with this internal endeavor. Our spiritual work this month is blessed by 11's celestial vibration, one of Numerology's master numbers. Otherworldly energy is present within this number. Eleven helps us learn a life lesson through the vibration's focus on actualization of spiritual principles in human form. Energy used for spiritual actualization brings excitement and vibrancy to the effort. There is a tingling expectancy that captivates and encourages us onward.

The planet Neptune influences this master number when residing in our Sun kissed sign of the month, Scorpio. November's quest deepens emotionally and spiritually under Scorpio's mysterious nature. Neptune's environmental focus also adds weight to the overall purpose of living in season with nature to correct the mistakes we have made. It sets us on a different environmental course. Interestingly, Neptune, master number 11 and Scorpio share a heightened intuitive awareness creating yet another link to our spiritual work of connecting with the collective consciousness. Intuition is the inner conduit between the spirit and human self. The more free our human vessel is of mildewed specks of life the more clear and accessible our intuition becomes.

Other attributes of Scorpio can help us strengthen our intuitive voice to better communicate with the Great Mother. Scorpio is an intensely passionate, idealistic and powerful sign. When pointed in the right direction Scorpio's energy digs deep to discover the relationship between universal and personal truth. This sign can be a bit of a zealot however, commanding us to live a highly principled life. Scorpio suffers no fools and is good for shaking up the status quo which helps with endeavors requiring a different perspective. Our quest, although aided by Scorpio, needs a little tempering to survive the journey unscathed, and sting free.

Citrine, one of November's birthstones is the perfect complement and foil for Scorpio and lends a gentleness to our spiritual journey this month. This stone is a good example of the power of goodwill. It serves to remind us that positive force outweighs an equal measure of negative force. Citrine emits a benevolent and generous energy that attracts wealth and abundance to the wearer. For this reason, it's referred to as the merchant's stone. Through its eternal optimism it counteracts negativity by sensing and releasing dark emotions hidden in the deep recesses of our being. Citrine will also help us discover those things for which we are grateful that lie beneath the surface. Awareness and gratitude of life's gems helps connect us to the bounty of the Great Mother.

The spiritual tasks of the month are deeply rooted in the mysterious connections of life. So too is Feng Shui. Our work this month and the ritual are aided by this ancient tradition. Specifically, the energy of Chen, the I Ching trigram influencing the Health & Family Bagua. This Bagua helps build a solid foundation by shoring up our internal and external supports. The supports are both people that affirm our best interest as well as choices that serve a healthy and pleasurable lifestyle. Life is stormy. Our foundation helps us survive the winds of change. Once calm is restored, we may experience our hard earned fulfillment and consider the existential meaning of life's joys and hardships.

Prepare for November's Ritual

If possible, perform the ritual around Thanksgiving.

~ Seasonings for the Wise Hazel Tree's November Brew ~

For the Ritual Altar~

An Altar Cloth

Brown and Ocher Candles for Mother Earth and Father Sky

A Smudge Stick of Sage

A Bowl to Withstand the Fire's Flames

Stone of Citrine for November's Intent

To Stand Next to a Symbol for Spirit

A Horn of Plenty Basket

A Goddess Habondia Doll

A Book of Plenty

Gourds and Harvest Corn

Leaves, Pine Needles and Acorn Hats Gathered While Out and About

Your Wand Made from a Stick

Hazelnut Coffee and a Bowl of Nuts

Tasks Before the Ritual

1. Make a *Book of Plenty*~ Use stationary on hand or buy recycled paper. On November 1st, begin a daily page of gratitude. Be as specific as possible, the length is up to you. Allow for an expansive collection of gratitude even digging through the layers of your life to unearth neglected areas for which you are thankful. Place the daily pages of thanks into the Horn of Plenty basket which is placed in the Health & Family Bagua of the home or room. On the last day of the month, make your *Book of Plenty* from the pages of gratitude. Bind the book in any way that suits you.

2. Fashion a doll to represent Habondia, the Goddess of Abundance

3. Take a walk at dusk~ observe the dance of color of light on leaves, hear the absence of birds, listen to the rustle of squirrels racing through autumn's groundcover, and the wind sailing through barren trees.

4. Take another walk or two and gather nuggets from nature~ leaves, pine needles and acorn hats. Drop shelled nuts along the way for Mother's foraging creatures.

5. Offer thanks before meals to the Great Mother for life's bounty. A prayer of your liking or this one will do~

Great Mother~ Giver of life,

From Your Hands to Mine,

I Accept this Offering

of Abundance

and Offer a Grateful Heart in Return.

6. Rake a snake path through the leaves making a big pile of leaves at the end. Race down the path and jump in the leaves or invite a youngin to play~ remembering a time when fallen leaves were fun.

7. As you make ready for winter, ponder nature's equivalent. How do the personal and outer worlds reflect one another?

8. Listen to your intuition~ When does your inner voice speak, what does it say? Try following its lead.

9. Find a charm symbolizing your gratefulness and attach to the wand.

The Day of the Ritual

Prepare the Ritual Feast~

Place your favorite nuts in an earthen bowl or basket. Be sure to use your charged water to brew your Hazelnut coffee. Hazelnut comes in many versions: as a syrup, flavored coffee beans and in powder form.

Placement of the Altar~

Lay the altar cloth on the table

For the Four Directions~

Wand in the East

Sage and burning Bowl in the South

Coffee and nuts in the West

Inside the Horn of Plenty basket put the gourds, harvest corn, leaves, pine needles,

acorn hats and place the basket in the North next to the Goddess Habondia doll

Place the brown and ocher candles in the center to represent Mother Earth and Father Sky

Stand the symbol for spirit before the candles

Lay the Citrine stone on top of the *Book of Plenty* and

place the book next to the coffee and nuts

Add other offerings of gratitude if you wish

Time to Center and Smudge~

Cast the Circle~

Invite the Directions~

Reader:

Welcome Direction of East, Spirit of Intuition. Discover the language of your wisdom ~
hear the difference between your voice and divine's ~ follow the insight, see where it leads.

Welcome Direction of South, Spirit of Manifestation. Light from within the fire
of abundance ~ the acceptance of worth ~ the courage to live a full life.

Welcome Direction of West, Spirit of Gratefulness. Happen upon a
state of grace ~ lightly, joyfully ~ like a child who awakens in expectant
wonder and simple appreciation for what the day may bring.
(Have a taste of the Mother's treats.)

Welcome Direction of North, Spirit of Harvest Plenty. Prepare as nature does
for the quiet stillness ahead ~ store nuts and blessings ~ wrap hovels and
homes in blankets of warmth ~ secure in the threads that hold us together.

Welcome Mother Earth and Father Sky. Autumn closes as darkness envelops
the day ~ barren trees stand silent in the absence of birds who sing elsewhere
~ All is well ~ much needed rest in the Mother's womb is coming.
Light the brown and ocher candles.

Carolann Gregoire, MSW

The Winds of Habondia

Blown in by the Goddess of Abundance

Reader, recite as Goddess Habondia:

Dark touches day turning light into dusk.

Change slips in at twilight.

Fallen leaves,

barren trees

make French silk silhouettes.

Rolling carpets of luscious green

lay underneath

rustling layers of scarlet tinted brown.

Pools of water refreshing in summer

spill into autumn scented baths.

The winds of change

turn toil into harvest

And

cause for celebration!

The winds of Habondia

blow finished specks of life away

making room

for the future

And

A Grateful Heart!

A Plentiful Life

A Dedication

Reader, instruct the stewards to hold their *Book of Plenty* next to their heart.

Reader, We invite Habondia, the Goddess of Abundance and Prosperity to bless our book of gratitude. Recite as Habondia:

Pages, 30 in all.

Each different from the other,

obvious and less so.

A month to ponder the goodness of life,

to measure the fullness of existence.

Awareness, surprise, dismay,

thoughts, awakenings,

emotions evoked.

Not always easy to discover the good.

Hidden treasures mined below the surface

dug deep, deeper still,

to unearth the forgotten.

Return to now

fuller than yesterday,

changed from the quest to discover our good.

Pages, 30 in all.

A reminder, to live life half full~ or more.

Reader, invite the stewards to read a page from their Book of Plenty and share the experience of discovering their plentiful life.

Oneness With the Great Mother

Meditation~

Reader:

At times, alone, disconnected from others, at odds with the source.

Recognize the moments of aloneness and oneness,

the difference in touch, duration and impact.

Distinguish between solitary union and loneliness.

Humans feel loneliness ~ Souls sense solitary union.

We need each other ~ humans and souls.

Out of touch humans too easily fall into darkness.

Souls on earth desire human expression.

Entwined as one yet distant in communion,

find a way to meet.

Speak in language common to both.

Live the interdependence natural to us all.

Joining, connecting within brings energy and power untapped alone.

Once connected, solitary union takes hold.

Roots begin to reach out to those nearby.

Well formed roots ~ solid and sturdy,

entwining in embrace and accommodation of others.

Roots of different textures accepted without question.

Rejoicing separately and together in abundant times,

helping and being helped during lean times.

Feel your roots connected with others reaching down through the earth,

to the source, the Great Mother.

Rest upon her belly,

wash up in cool waters, replenish from Her cupboard,

rise back to the surface once energy is restored.

Solitary Union

Sustained through a Common Language,

Connected with Others and the Source,

Stewards of the Great Mother!

Open the Circle~

Once you have finished the feast you may open the circle after offering

thanks to our guests for their protection and blessings ~

Mother Earth and Father Sky

the 4 Directions

Goddess Habondia

<u>After the Ritual</u>

Continue adding a page of gratitude till the end of the month. Then bind the pages together and place your finished *Book of Plenty,* symbol for spirit, and the Citrine stone in the Health & Family Bagua of the home or room for continued blessings of abundance. Return to the book when life feels half full or less.

All is Well in the Fall of the Leaves

~ Blessed Be ~

All is Well in the Stillness of her Womb

Winter~ A Time To:

Trust the Sun's Return ~ December

Rest With the Soul ~ January

Welcome Your Bliss ~ February

A Winter Essay

The first truly cold day is a jolt to the system. Our breath catches as chilly wisps of air familiar with our body find their way to our cold spot. Once rediscovered, this spot becomes a prominent indwelling point of wintry sensation. It can be an uncomfortable season especially, if either by choice or draft, our home is nippy as well. The harsh elements of winter encase us within an icy awareness of the season's risk to our existence. This sensual acuity acts as a behavioral grounding force ensuring our survival.

Cold is cold, there is no denying winter's bone chilling weather. However, the temperature can be tempered a bit by our response. Winter, more than any other season, challenges our mental capacity to embrace the difficult. If we successfully meet this challenge, it can positively alter our experience. Children instinctually understand the power of mind over matter. Unjaded by the chilly reality, they delight in the magic of winter's wonderland. Little ones are our teachers in these matters. They lead through example to the simple pleasure of receiving the joyful gifts of the season.

At first glance, the season's landscape looks oppressive and dreary and seemingly devoid of color and life. Yet, winter can be a lovely time of the year. Winter's quiet muse floats softly around and through the stark contrasting colors of light and dark contributing to the lyrical feel of the season. The dark brown silhouette of trees alongside winter white is actually quite beautiful. Stripped of their leaves, we can better admire their artistic lines. Snow affords us play time outside on slopes, icy ponds and sledding hills. Warming up in front of a fire after a playful outing fills the heart. The ability to return home to a warm and loving hearth is one of the season's wishes.

The eye catches very little movement afoot as winter is the sleeping time in the natural world. Perhaps, it's the stillness that evokes such unease with the season. We don't sit well in silence. Our challenge this season is to trust in the Great Mother's winter design. There is purpose to the seeming lifelessness of nature. It's a time to drift deep within the self and experience winter's stillness. While we await the return of the Sun, rest in slippered feet within the Mother's womb. The opportunity for greatness arises from a period of rest with the soul. The inspired inklings of our next masterpiece need space in stillness to germinate. Once restored, the human spirit is more easily inspired. Intuition is more accessible enabling the human self to hear our heart's desire. All is Well in the Stillness of Her Womb.

Chapter 4

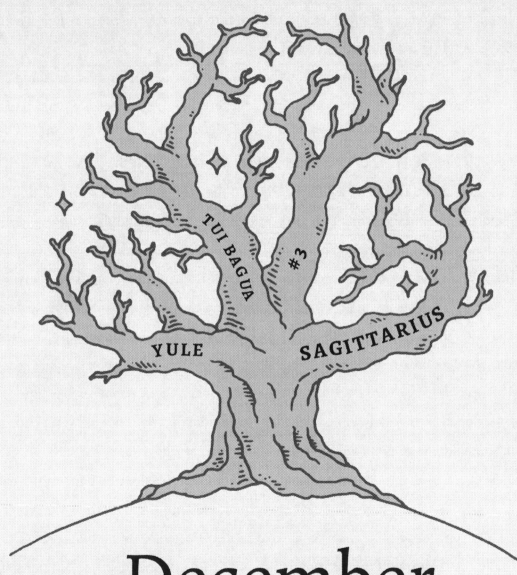

December

Trust the Sun's Return

December's Sensual Nature

The look and feel of winter takes hold overnight, confounding the reality that fall remains with us until the end of the month when the Mother turns the wheel at Winter Solstice. Looking out frosted windows, the outdoor scene is coated in a soft white glaze. The trees are bare, the sky is gray and the temperature drops. It takes awhile to warm up to the cold after being caught off guard by the abrupt turn in mercury. Getting out of a warm, cozy bed is put off until the last possible moment to delay the morning shivers. It takes longer to get out the door after pulling on boots and hunting for scarves and gloves. Once out the door, another shock wave of cold hits as we race to the car to start it up. By the time the car is warmed up we're often where we were headed and back out again into the cold. Early December is a test of wills between the chill and our resistance to it. The quicker we give in, the faster our bodies adjust and settle into the season's shorter days and long, chilly nights.

Thankfully, December's joyful beauty prompts us to embrace the change in seasons. It is a month to enjoy. Snowflakes foretell snow days from school and snowmen in the front yard. The first snow is mesmerizing as we look up with arms and legs spread wide in welcome of the Mother's wispy flakes. With eyes skyward, we take in the falling snow encasing the trees in snowy tufts. Then, shifting our gaze, we trace the horizon and behold Her earthy patchwork of brown and white. There is beauty in the sharp angled, minimalist landscape of the Great Mother's still and quiet time.

Decorative winter and holiday displays remind us December is an honored month. Suiting its status, the month is cloaked in a jeweled robe of holy proportions. Winter is on glorious display throughout the royal month of December. We dress the outside in merry cheer hanging twinkling lights on houses, trees, and shrubs. Our efforts serve to reflect December's magical glow and deflect our attention away from the absence of the Sun's light. Candlelight observance has become a shared element of many December holidays such as the Christian's advent wreath, Hanukkah's menorah, and Kwanzaa's kinaras. These culturally diverse candles share a similar purpose; they shine light upon their tradition's spiritual center. Wreaths of holly and pinecones are draped on doors to welcome friends and family into our adorned homes. Doors open to rooms transformed by celestial music and the majestic presence of the evergreen. Boxes of decorations provide hours of amusement. Heirlooms and family favorites are rediscovered evoking funny, uplifting and sometimes misty memories of holidays past. Treasured ornaments are placed with care creating enchanted scenes of make believe. Transfixed, our homes captivate our imagination and whisk us away to distant times and old world traditions.

We delight our family and friends with foods bursting with savory decadence. Dog eared and butter stained recipes passed down from one generation to the next are dusted off and propped up on kitchen counters cluttered with culinary wizardry. Dishes cooked with cinnamon, nutmeg and vanilla mix with the green, earthy aroma of Christmas and Yule, the Winter Solstice. Resistance is futile. We put away plates of homemade cookies and cakes, bowls of gooey candy, baskets of fruit and cheese and boxes of chocolate covered cherries. Surprisingly, after all our snacking, we still have room for sumptuous, hearth prepared suppers. Afterwards, we unwind in front of a wood burning fire with a cup of coffee or an occasional hot rum toddy. Giving ourselves permission to indulge reminds us that holiday cheer tastes good going down and rests easy on the soul. Our tummies full, we can relax into a joyful state of wonderment.

Later in the month we will experience the darkest nite of the year amidst the candle lit festivities. The saving grace of this nite is heralded at daybreak when we begin the journey back to the Sun. Spiritually, this rebirth of the Sun God is a multi-cultural celebration. Elders of many traditions foretell a similar story of a son born to a virgin mother. The annual telling affirms the universal promise of radiant Sun filled grace. The Great Mother invites us to listen to the story in the language of our spirit and trust in this ancient promise as old as Father time.

A Visit to the Wise Hazel Tree

On a dark, Moonless night, the Wise Hazel Tree listens. Bare limbs outstretched in wait. The steward moves closer to the Tree, robed in winter layers from head to foot, arms wrapped around Her trunk for warmth. A distant noise disturbs the stillness. They stir expectedly. And, wait… for the trumpet to sound again…proclaiming the return of Her Sun.

Branches of December's Wise Hazel Tree

Yule~ Winter Solstice

Tui~ Children & Creativity Bagua

Vibration of 3

Sun in Sagittarius

The month shimmers in expectant joy at the rebirth of the Sun God. Civilizations across time and space have honored and worshipped the star. It's no wonder. We can't live without his golden glow. We depend on the Sun for both physical and spiritual sustenance. Without the Sun's radiance, our lives are cold, desolate, lifeless. The star brings light, warmth and growth to all living things. Even those of us who appreciate the cast of the Moon's shadow begin to feel down and insecure during the dark months.

Sun centered holy days arise from our need to entice the Sun's return, to feel his presence upon our face. The Sun's exulted glory is a cornerstone of many spiritual traditions. Cultures both ancient and contemporary lovingly tell a similar tale of rebirth reflecting our shared belief in the Sun King's triumphant arrival upon the earth. As evolving souls, we have returned to this story since time immortal just as the wheel turns to face the Sun. Sighing in relief, we rejoice in celebration. Resting easier, we settle into winter with the feel of the Sun Lord once again upon our back.

With the spread of Christianity, Jesus became a ruling Sun God and has hence enjoyed an enduring reign. Prior to Jesus, another called Mithras was worshipped across civilizations. They shared in common their birth to a virgin mother and promise of eternal existence. Christmas traditions today and Yule customs of old both herald our desire to honor our King. Their commonality exemplifies efforts of the early Christian church to convert pagans to the flock by absorbing traditional elements of the earth based religion. The Winter Solstice is perhaps the most obvious. Edain McCoy, tells us the evergreen, holiday plants, wreaths, sleigh rides, and gift giving that symbolize the Christian holy day are reminiscent of pagan lore.

Decorating with winter's raw elements is an ancient Celtic custom. The evergreen was a natural choice. This tree maintains its color throughout the season, most noticeably during winter when we desperately need a glimpse of green. Ornaments of wishes were hung on this festive and sacred tree similar to our New Year's resolutions. Wreaths, an enduring symbol of the wheel of life throughout the seasons, are adorned for Yule with pinecones. The union of the masculine (pinecone) and feminine (wreath) symbolize another promise made in winter, the future mating of the God and Goddess. The Yule log is another symbol of their unified dual energies when candles representing the triple Goddess are placed inside the phallic log.

Even Santa and his sleigh ride across the night sky delivering presents to the children of the world on Christmas Eve resembles other pagan stories, such as that of Frau Holde. She is a German Goddess believed to have delivered gifts from a sky driven sleigh. One of the most interesting examples of pagan lore influencing contemporary fables is the tale of the Holly King and the Oak King. The precursors to Santa and his reindeer can be found in the contest of these Kings. Their seasonal conflict erupts twice a year at Midwinter and Midsummer. At Yule, the Oak King defeats his foe and enjoys his reign until Midsummer when he is summarily overthrown by the Holly King. Their reigns, each half a year long, help turn the Great Mother's wheel of life. Santa's suit of red, and reindeer driven sleigh are reminiscent of the Holly King's red robe, and herd of eight deer.

There is one more delightful carryover from ancient pagan customs, which is found in the origin of our Christmas plants, the Holly and Mistletoe. Both are attributed to their adornment of the pagan Kings and celebration at their wheel turning contests. Mystical mistletoe is also beloved because of its romantic allure. The plant's purported magical properties has contributed to its long and festive history. Supposedly, couples who kiss underneath its bough of soft white blossoms will find lasting love. This symbol of love's endurance reflects an even deeper purpose. With the birth of the Sun God at Yule, we are assured of the eventual union of the God and Goddess.

Yule, is such a rich holiday. It is a time of rebirth, reunion of the God and Goddess and the welcomed turn towards the Sun. Our spirits soar, voices are raised in song and eyes open to the wonder and joy of life. Yule is an invitation to step outside of our daily lives and experience a world of innocence. It's a community where faith, bliss and peace reside. Secure in our belief that the wheel will turn towards the light affords us the opportunity to pause and breathe deeply, and to allow bliss and peace the time to burrow in through our human veneer and dress our spirit in holiday cheer. The longer we reside in this world of innocence the more able we are to welcome the new year with hope and purpose.

Traditions from our Wise Hazel Tree fall along nicely with December's spiritual expression of hope, faith, and joy. We begin with Feng Shui. The Children & Creativity Bagua was chosen for this majestic month because of the influence of the I Ching trigram, Tui. The Bagua draws its energy from this trigram's emphasis on child-like innocence and joy. The Bagua reminds us to live life in daily wonder, to create from the heart and to love ourselves and others unconditionally. Activating this Bagua's energy helps us maintain our belief in miracles long past the boxing up of holiday trimmings.

Sagittarius, the Sun kissed sign of December is the perfect complement to this holiday month. Sagittarius is first in line as the Holly King carries us away in a sleigh of reindeer to a land of fables and make believe and old world sensibilities. As the zodiac philosopher, those under its influence are explorers of ideas. Keepers of the sign are busy and restless spirits that delight in the search for meaning and purpose. Known as the archer, the sign takes aim and follows the arrow's release into unknown realms. Sagittarius takes a light hearted approach to adventure and expects a positive end to all endeavors. As there is much to explore and understand, the energy of this sign is direct, cutting through to the heart of the matter. Like Scorpio, Sagittarius suffers no fools. Thankfully, its fun loving energy tempers the sign's idealistic nature and passionate displays.

Although serious, Yule has a joyful and generous undercurrent which contributes to our excited anticipation of the holiday. Numerology as well as Astrology influence the spirit of the season with the vibration of number 3. Social and friendly in focus, the number underscores the giving and kindhearted element of Yule festivities. Generosity flows effortlessly from hearts in communion with spirit. Turquoise, Sagittarius's companion stone guides us to this place of spiritual union. The energy of the stone, ancient in use, encourages the soul's expression in a loving and peaceful way. Like its Sun sign friend, strong and vibrant Turquoise helps us explore the core fundamental truths of the universe, of life itself.

However understood, the majesty of this holy day strikes a chord deep within us reverberating a single joyous note around the world. For this we may be grateful. In days to come we may learn to accept the different tellings as variations of the same spiritual message. For this we may be hopeful. It's because of these gifts of hope, joy, and peace our beloved month holds an honored place within the season of winter. Nestled within holly adorned trees with the Sun at its back, royal December shines again, opening our hearts in joyful innocence and restoring our faith in the Sun's return.

<u>Prepare for December's Ritual</u>

If possible, perform the ritual at Yule, the Winter Solstice.

~ Seasonings for the Wise Hazel Tree's December Brew ~

For the Ritual Altar~

An Altar Cloth

A Handmade Yule Log with Three Silver Candles

A Scarlet Candle for Mother Earth and Father Time

A Smudge Stick of Sage

A Bowl to Withstand the Fire's Flames

Stone of Turquoise for December's Intent

To Stand Next to a Symbol for Spirit

A Mother Earth Doll

A Basket of Pinecones for New Year Wishes

Bits of Nature Gathered While Out and About

Favorite Holiday Ornaments

Your Wand Made from a Stick

Spiced Cider and Pound Cake Drizzled with Your Favorite Red Topping

<u>Tasks Before the Ritual</u>

1. In the Children & Creativity Bagua of your bedroom place a purple candle to be lit while reading, *A Visit to Midwinter Manor*, a tale of the King's return. Read once a week (or as often as you like) at bedtime and watch the magic unfold the next morn.

A Visit to Midwinter Manor
as Told by the Olde Bard, Carolan

Hark,

Spirits of Joy,

Faeries of Goodwill,

light upon my heart this morn.

Turn this day from dark to light.

Carolann Gregoire, MSW

Show me the way to the land of wonder.

Deep into the forest I gaily go,

with my winged companions of cheer.

Walking upon the snow covered path in slippers laced in gold,

wearing robes spun by maidens in wait and cut in shimmering royal green,

guided by candle lit trees strung with garlands of holly.

The Robin whispers~ Trust the way to the Manor

as our footsteps take us deeper into the woods

until,

transfixed by Midwinter's magic,

the Manor stands aglow!

Protected behind and on either side by the Great Mother's work.

Cloaked in tapestries of silk that grace the ground from turrets above,

with scenes of joy and peace woven from hundreds of berry stained threads.

To delight the senses

and, keep winter's chill at bay.

Look who awaits, who greets at the gate with sweeping bow.

The Holly King, sleigh packed and harnessed with deer.

Off to encircle the Globe on his last nite of reign,

bestowing to all

his Goodwill and cheer.

The Holly King takes flight as we bid adieu

and the Manor door now Oak opens wide,

carved with words of welcome in ancient Ogham script.

We enter, my companions and I

to radiant firelight scented with ancient brews,

heady and warm to turn our attention within.

The eyes take in the great hall adorned in mistletoe

and orbiting purple spheres.

Swaying from rope of silver fir,

braided by her familiar, the Mother's sprite.

Zinfandel paned windows lit by cobalt's flame cast the hall in a rose blush,

settling upon a grand table spanning the hall laden in feast befitting a King's welcome.

Surrounded by friends and family from here and beyond.

Aromas stirring our hunger,

meat pies, plum cherry jelly, tarts and warm crusty bread.

Time skips a beat,

a hush befalls

an exquisite sigh bursts from our lips,

as we turn and behold The Oak King,

standing between Towers of Evergreen.

"Come my children, the Oak King beckons with arms ready for embrace.

Tis the season of Joy, Light and Peace,

join with me and yours, make merry and feast.

My gift, blessed in days of light awaits your turn."

Joy fills the heart as winter's muse, the bellowing laughter and soft tinkling of bells is heard.

Performed by a royal team of deer across this solstice eve night

as the sturdy, protective door of the Midwinter Manor closes and the feast of Yule begins.

2. Arise at daybreak on the Winter Solstice and welcome the Sun's return, observing his ascent in silence.

3. Dress the altar doll to represent Mother Earth.

4. Make a Yule log for the ritual. Go to a wooded area and find a small log twelve inches or less (Oak is preferable). Or, check with stalls selling Christmas trees. The cut off portion of the trunk would work and is a green way to honor the discarded portion of this sacred tree. Drill three holes to hold the three silver candles to complete this symbol of fertility and the reunion of the Goddess and the God. Leave the log plain or decorate it with holly, mistletoe, or other seasonal greenery.

5. Find a day or two to walk and enjoy the look of barren trees against the Mother's winter landscape. Gather bits of nature for the altar and scatter nuts for our furry friends.

6. Discover a simple offering of peace. The gesture, a making of your own design.

7. Find a charm symbolizing one aspect of the holiday and attach it to the wand.

The Day of the Ritual

Prepare the Ritual Feast~

To honor an old pagan tradition of offering cake and ale at this Midwinter

feast, we shall offer pound cake and spiced cider to our ethereal and

corporal guests. Brew your own spiced cider or use a packaged spice ball.

Store bought cake is fine~ drizzled with your favorite red topping.

Placement of the Altar~

Lay the altar cloth on the table

For the Four Directions~

Wand in the East

Sage and burning bowl in the South

Cake and cider in the West

Basket of pinecones in the North

In the center of the altar arrange the Yule log and silver candles,

the stone of Turquoise for December's intent next to

Your symbol for spirit,

and the scarlet candle, our symbol for Mother Earth and Father Time

Scatter bits of nature around the basket of pinecones

Place the Mother Earth doll near the basket of pinecones

Place the holiday ornaments where you wish

Time to Center and Smudge~

Cast the Circle~

Invite the Directions~

Reader:

Welcome Direction of East, Spirit of Good Tidings. Foretold blessings await! Faith,

trust, belief in the Sun's inevitable return. Open to the wonder. Embrace the promise.

Welcome Direction of South, Spirit of Rebirth. Mary~ Goddess, Mother of
Prophet Jesus. Sacred womb, noble spirit, holy commitment. Raised her Sun
with wisdom, love and courage. Fierce protectress of eternal grace.

Welcome Direction of West, Spirit of Giving. Awaken from slumber. Innocence
intact. Hearts swell~ spilling and flowing into another's. The touch of kindness
felt around the world. The sound of bells drifts into the distance.
(Have a taste of cake and ale.)

Welcome Direction of North, Spirit of Ancient Stories. Preserved for
us by Crones, Priests, and Elders entrusted with the telling of hallowed
traditions to restore hope and a joyful spirit to their people.

Welcome Mother Earth and Father Time. We rejoice with you on this most sacred nite
when the wheel turns towards the Sun. The story resonant with the soul is heard igniting a
power made great by our solitary union. Together we survey the changed tenor of the land.
Light the scarlet candle.

A Tribute to the Sun's Return

Reader:

The Sun, Power of our Planet
the beginning of all life, ignited by this Star.
Rays~ vibrant, warm, worshipped,
shine upon all
regardless.
Wondrous and expected,
spiritual traditions evolving to symbolize
our salvation through the Sun's grace.
Mythical understandings told in different tongues
as close to the truth as humans can tell.
Presumably, there were others before Mithras,
recurring Sun Gods,

some virgin born, always mystical.

Draped in mystery and high secrets to protect

and draw us in.

Spiritual evolution makes room for another Sun God

to summon us to contemporary grace.

The Sun's return in Jesus, a baby

born to Mary, raised by Joseph

in a land of many stories.

Challenges us to coexist in peace,

feed the hungry,

treat each other as equals,

speak against hypocrisy

And love, Always love!

An Incantation for the Reunion of the Lord and Lady
a Yule log spell

Reader:

Lord and Lady, lovers divided

separated by death at All Hallow's Eve.

Powers Unite once more

tonite at Midwinter Solstice.

The oaken log, symbol of Yule,

the Great Mother's consort, her Sun God

strong and virile,

faithful in his promised return,

join now with the Triple Goddess,

the Lady Moon.

Loneliness abates

as lips rediscover pleasure.

Caress the face of the Maiden, your first love.

Joyful, innocent playmate,

teacher of unconditional love.

Embrace her lighthearted spirit, her trusting ways.

Steward, light the silver candle on the left.

Turn now to face the Mother, bearer of future Suns.

Sensual, eager lover of Yule,

fierce protectress of the young.

Embrace her wildness, her fearless stand.

Steward, light the silver candle in the middle.

Behold the face of the Crone, lined in wisdom.

Steadfast partner through life,

resolute keeper of the mysteries.

Embrace her just and knowing heart.

Steward, light the silver candle on the right.

Sun Lord and Lady Moon,

separate powers

united once more at Midwinter Solstice.

Forever

symbols of Enduring Love!

Wishes for the New Year

a Granting Spell

Reader, recite as the steward:

Fortuna, Goddess of Good Luck,

Jupiter, God of Good Fortune,

deities of roman splendor,

I stand in your presence.

My heart humbled by

the season's celestial gifts.

I come before the year's end,

seeking your blessing upon my wishes of goodwill.

To invoke

your magick, your power to make real

that which serves my highest good,

and soul's desire.

Tales of your reign

majestic and benevolent,

treasured by the pagan,

bring me to you.

With Crowns of Glory

stunning in Turquoise and Ruby,

gems of stature

befitting your grandeur,

grant my soul's desire.

My requests, sincere for

Indwelling Peace

Protected Diversity

Safe and Warm beds

Full Bellies

Expansive Minds

Cultural Understanding

Spiritual Unfolding

Endless Well-being

Joyful Days, Loving Nites

And

Respect for Mother Earth.

Reader, invite the stewards to write out their personal wishes and add them to the basket of pinecones, a symbol of fertility. If comfortable, read them aloud first.

Reader, recite as Goddess Fortuna and God Jupiter:

My Child, We Hear

the longing of your soul,

the timbre of your heart.

Your requests,

honorable and just

will be Granted

in the New Year

through your diligence

and the Blessings of the Goddess Fortuna and God Jupiter.

Open the Circle~

Once you have finished the feast and merry making offer thanks

to the four directions and our other noble guests~

Mother Mary

Goddess Fortuna

Triple Goddess

Mother Earth

Father Time

the Olde Bard, Carolan

God Jupiter

Oak King

Holly King

Winged companions

Mithras

and baby Jesus

<u>After the Ritual</u>

Stewards, on New Year's Day release your wishes. Light the divine scarlet candle, read your list aloud and recite:

My Child, We Hear

the longing of your soul,

the timbre of your heart.

Your requests,

honorable and just

will be Granted

in the New Year

through your diligence

and the blessings of the Goddess Fortuna and God Jupiter.

Release them to God Jupiter and Goddess Fortuna by the candle's flame.

Place the Turquoise stone and symbol for spirit in the Children & Creativity

Bagua of the home or room for your return to innocence and wonder.

All is Well in the Stillness of Her Womb

~ Blessed Be ~

Chapter 5

January

Rest With the Soul

January's Sensual Nature

The reckoning of the season dawns in January, the first month of the Gregorian calendar. In the absence of a holiday to occupy our attention we can no longer deny the presence of winter. Trees no longer strung with lights reveal their simple beauty and purpose, to shelter nature amidst their slender branches. The treetops once bushy now house round leaf balls of nesting squirrels. Knots in trees and hollowed stumps become home to all manner of sleeping creatures and the faerie folk of childhood fables. Walks offer a different view of the neighborhood. The invisible becomes visible as houses, hidey holes and other formations no longer hidden behind a natural screen come into view.

Our vision lifts becoming panoramic without the fullness of nature to tantalize our senses below. The splendor of night, quiet and starkly beautiful is unveiled in January. The now familiar riveting cold stills our pace, causing us to pause long enough to search the evening sky. Stars sparkle and pop as their reflection bounces off a white, snow covered earth. The curved contours of the Crescent Moon are more distinct against a black velvet sky. Our impulse to pluck these jewels from the sky intensifies. Our desire to turn them into celestial talismans to warm the skin and inspire the spirit is within our grasp in January.

The new year for many reminds us of all the things we want to do and haven't done. A list of well intentioned resolutions is a good strategy, but foolhardy to attempt in the stillness of the month. Reflection sits well in cool stillness, implementation runs better in warm weather. Living in season in contemporary society is difficult to achieve in winter. Life goes on, work remains hectic, the juggle of roles seems relentless. When we peek outside our lives we tend to be in direct opposition to what is occurring naturally. But, if we can let go and relax into the month, January offers us thirty-one days of cozy comfort.

Enjoy the outdoors, but don't miss winter's indoor purpose, to drink mugs of peppermint tea and hot chocolate, wrapped in thick hand knit throws and indulge in fun shaped cookies sprinkled with sugary glitter placed enticingly atop one another on a beveled glass plate. Winter foods like steaming bowls of slow cooked recipes abate winter's chill. Meals simmered in slow cookers always deliver in taste what teased the nose all day long. Winter meals seem more nourishing and satisfying, perhaps, because aromas don't have to compete as much with the other senses this time of year. At home, books we've put off reading come back into sight, nights open to more family time for watching old black and white movies or new releases. Board games stir up friendly sibling competition. Outdoor recreation aside, there does seem to be more of a pull to indoors and creative ways to have fun and spend time together. After all, it is chilly outside.

The icy crispness of January's bracing winds chafe our skin leaving a bone deep rawness. Our shivers of vulnerability actually refresh and fortify this outer layer of protection. Warm and safe within, our spirit brushes off the chill and settles in for a slumbering soulful sleep. There is a gentleness about January that feels like a sleepy Sunday. Not much happens in January, this month of rest. It's within this middle month of winter when we may finally give in to our inclination to rest slippered feet upon worn, leathered ottomans and close our eyes to the world.

A Visit to the Wise Hazel Tree

The Wise Hazel Tree dark limbed and wet with snow, speaks in hushed tones lest she wakens her keep. "Look at my uppermost branch on the right she whispers, see what swings in the icy breeze." The steward sees the swaying of what looks to be a silver pendant molded by fire, hanging from a cord sinewy and black as night. The Tree tells the steward, "It's a gift from my daughter, Princess Periwinkle of the Crescent Moon. Winter is her favorite time of the year. She remembered my stories of January, told when she was young and engraved them into this pendant. Slip the necklace over your head and lay beneath blankets of down in this bed hollowed from a stump. I'll keep watch as you sleep. All is well~ January's story will be told as winter's stillness unfolds."

Branches of January's Wise Hazel Tree

The Raven

K'un~ Love & Relationship Bagua

Vibration of 1

Sun in Capricorn

Fewer distractions allow for time and space to slip into the magick of stillness, the spiritual gift of the month. Our spirit naturally dwells within a sanctuary of peace co-created with the source, the Great Mother. Our human self craves this den of serene calm that we seldom get to experience. To our conscious mind, a tranquil state of being seems illusive and unattainable. We fear its implication of relinquished control and fall into a nothingness abyss, doomed to an aimless existence. Our waking consciousness takes its responsibility for our survival on earth quite seriously and is very cautious in handing the reins over to something or someone else. That's good. There's nothing wrong with a little caution to keep us out of harm's way.

But, what does it really mean to have peace of mind. Part of our problem of not having it seems to be a cultural misunderstanding of the concept. On the positive side, Americans are rugged explorers, dreamers and high achievers through hard, sustained work. The downside of our cultural nature is our tendency to conquer, tame and bend others to our will. In contrast, the concept of tranquility feels lightweight, effortless, a tad bit lazy and slow. Even for industrialized nations we move very fast, constantly. For many Americans, the act of a peaceful mind is a foreign and unfamiliar state of being.

Interestingly, the English dictionary uses the word "freedom", several times to describe a peaceful state of mind. Tranquility is explained as the freedom from noise, disturbance, conflict, and violence. At first glance these opponents of peace appear external. Yet, each has the capacity to disrupt the interior self. Living a picturesque existence is only as serene as our internal chatter is quiet. It's true that the outer world reflects our inner life. And, we do have far more control over our daily experience than we think we do. We can free ourselves from the internal barriers to a tranquil life.

It's time to ponder these questions. Is it possible to achieve a state of peace maintained over time? One hopes. Have we claimed peaceful living as evolving human spirits? Not yet.

But, it does feel like we are opening to the possibility, despite humanity's appalling behavior depicted repeatedly on the twenty-four hour news channels. There is a palpable yearning for less strife, less discord both inside and out. Optimistic idealism when fueled by necessity is a powerful impetus for change. Beginning this month, we can slip into the magick of stillness where peace of mind awakens by giving ourselves permission to rest with the soul and free ourselves of worldly distractions.

We turn to the ancient traditions to help us find this counterculture haven of inner peace. Beloved, duty bound Capricorn, our Sun kissed sign of January will gladly lend his hand to our spiritual work when asked. The strengths and challenges of this sign actually mirror those of American culture posed earlier, adding an exciting twist to the sign's involvement in our quest for peace. Capricorn's earthy and outward bound nature may not fully appreciate an inward journey, but will help none-the-less out of a sense of deep loyalty and a protective desire to keep us safe. We may be teased a bit and have to put up with a little chuckling, but that will help temper our sober journey with fun and light. Likewise, we are a generous people often helping outside our comfort zone without thought to our own risk. When the crisis is over we'll often brush off any attempt to describe our actions as heroic.

Like us, Capricorn is achievement oriented, working feverishly to see a goal through to its completion. It's this very astrological and cultural characteristic that takes us to the brink of exhaustion. We don't always know when to stop, but even when we do, we still may not give ourselves permission to breathe. We need to learn to use this incredibly focused, willful energy for inward journeying. The quest for inner peace takes a studied approach, one requiring commitment and discipline-- hard work. It's a lifetime practice of taking time to be still, sitting with spirit and acting upon inner wisdom. Take a moment to consider the global implications of personal tranquility. Imagine the far reaching impact of circles of peace emanating from Saturn's rings if we enlisted the help of this driven planetary task master. Inner peace on these terms is hardly a lazy man's choice of endeavors.

Discovering our inner haven is for many a trek into unknown territory. It's natural to feel a little unsure of our way. Snowflake Obsidian, Capricorn's talismanic stone, is wondrously outfitted for our inward quest. The look, name, and metaphysical attributes of this white on black stone couldn't be more perfect especially, pitched against January's black, starry sky.

Using this stone for our spiritual work will be enormously enlightening, particularly, its ability to protect, calm and soothe a weary soul. The stone will help center us in the right frame of mind to ponder and meditate.

Receptivity, the foundation for magick and meditative work is derived from feeling safe and secure. The combined attributes of Capricorn, Saturn and Snowflake Obsidian offer protection for traveling inward. As volcanic rock, Snowflake Obsidian's birth place is deep inside the Mother. Our meditative work this month is enhanced by this stone's ability to ground our physical body by running a conduit of energy from our base chakra to the center of the earth, the Mother's womb. Once anchored, our human self can relax, let go and allow our etheric body to rest with the soul.

As we yield to the pull within, our journey may open our eyes to painful aspects of our lives that need healing. Inner journeying often does. Our stone this month actually stimulates awareness of internal disharmony. If disharmony arises and it must be dealt with then, by all means, take care of yourself. Otherwise, simply take note of the discord. The intent of the month is rest and gentle self-care. Next month is a more spiritually appropriate time in which to take a closer look.

It's clear by this point that the middle month of winter opens the inner door of possibilities. Numerologically, number one, the symbol of new beginnings features in both new years: Gregorian January and Wiccan October. Wherein October was a community affair, the one in January is a solitary sojourn. The ancient traditions chosen for January all contain this aspect of aloneness. Fresh starts require preparation. K'un, the Love & Relationship Bagua activated for our spiritual work contains maternal energy according to Feng Shui author, Richard Webster. K'un is also referred to as, The Receptive. It is a loving and nurturing Bagua in which to help us center our energy on self-improvement. It also fosters the development of a closer relationship with our wise, high self.

Pathworking need not be fraught with trepidation. We have helpers and visionaries to guide us. We call upon the Raven. The animal totem known for his protective and prophetic powers. This magnificent black bird will show us the way to our inner sanctum. Once we've arrived we may rest safely within the Mother's womb. Later, much later, we will rise refreshed and ready to begin anew.

Prepare for January's Ritual

If possible, perform the ritual later in the month on a Saturday during

the dark, waning phase of the Moon. Saturdays are influenced by Saturn

and the dark Moon is a helpful time for meditative work.

~ Seasonings for the Wise Hazel Tree's January Brew ~

For the Ritual Altar~

An Altar Cloth

A Personal Symbol for Rest and Rejuvenation

A White Candle for Mother Earth and Father Sky

A Smudge Stick of Sage

A Cauldron to Withstand the Fire's Flames

Stone of Snowflake Obsidian for January's Intent

A Winter White Goddess Doll

To Stand Next to a Symbol of Spirit

White Paper and a Black Pen~ To Be Explained Later

A Slumberland Basket

Wintry Baubles for Merriment

A Peace Pendant Necklace

Peppermint Tea and Chocolate Cupcakes with Vanilla Frosting

Your Wand Made From a Stick

Tasks Before the Ritual

1. Clear the calendar~ eliminate as many shoulds as possible.

2. Treat yourself lightly with unlimited, simple expressions of self-love.

3. During walks look for wintry doorways into nature's slumberland.

4. Create a winter slumberland in a basket using bits of nature from your walks. If you make the slumberland before the ritual, place it in the love & relationship Bagua of your home or room.

5. Watch the Sun rise through the silhouette of a tree.

6. Dress the altar doll in winter white.

7. Make a peace pendant necklace using black, sinewy cord.

8. Attach a 'peace of mind' charm to the wand.

The Day of the Ritual

Prepare the Ritual Feast~

Winter cravings usually include yummy comfort treats. Peppermint tea

is comforting, refreshing and goes really well with chocolate. Be sure

to use your charged water for the tea. Embellish the wintry cupcake

with sprinkles or leave plain~ whichever your tummy desires.

Placement of the Altar~

Lay the altar cloth on the table

For the Four Directions~

Wand in the East

Sage and Cauldron in the South

Tea and Cupcake in the West

Slumberland Basket and the Winter White Goddess Doll in the North

In the center of the altar place the white candle for Mother Earth and Father Sky

Arrange the symbol for spirit and Snowflake Obsidian near the candles

Place the peace necklace in the east along with the paper and pen

Scatter your wintry baubles around the altar for merriment.

Time to Smudge~

Cast the Circle~

Invite the Directions~

Reader:

Welcome Direction of East, Spirit of Calming Thoughts. Moonlight quiet

spills from velvet skies onto Mother's winter white. Stillness spreads

as flakes descend~ slowing the pace, deepening the breath.

Welcome Direction of South, Spirit of Courage. Rings of Saturn encircle the inner plexus

with fired synergy. Cosmic immersion becomes solar fusion propelling us on our quest.

Welcome Direction of West, Spirit of Imagination. Tonite we open the
door to one of Her mysteries, the Mother's Slumberland. Dispel all
doubts that other worlds exist or risk being left at the door.
(Have a sip of tea and a frosty bite of cake.)

Welcome Direction of North, Spirit of Matter. The physical and ethereal
are both inhabited. Living in one~ dreaming in the other. Pathwork
joins them together~ a transcendent experience follows.

Welcome Mother Earth and Father Sky. The Mother's beauty stands stark upon
a hill, her silhouette becomes visible against the setting Sun and the rising stars.
She rests comfortably upon her land~ awaiting the magick of darkness.
Light the white candle.

Tulla Dannan, The Mother's Snowflake Faery

A Faery Story

(The tale came about with the help of Griffin Guinn)

Reader:

Upon waking one morn in times long ago,
the Great Mother felt listless, then bored, then listless some more.
The quiet, the chill so relentless this season
was taking its toll on her otherwise calm senses.
Grouchy and cranky she rolled out of bed
exposing herself to aloof icy breath.
Her slippers gone missing since Queen Maeve's last visit,
meant feet, baby bare, touched the cold and damp stone.
"Enough is enough," she barked and bellowed
while wrapping herself in quilt upon quilt,
till all could be seen were the tips of her toes.
"Brewing a fierce storm she was," Guinn recalls.
"Bring me Queen Maeve," she demanded of Guinn,

her broker of arrangements cast on a whim.

For Guinn had specialties born of his lineage

part faerie, half human, and a touch elfin some say.

~

Guinn set off in a hurry to Marsh Hollows and Maeve's castle

having witnessed before the Mother's ill temper.

The time when the gnomes in an effort to please

removed all the stars hoping the Mother would sleep. She didn't!

~

After a long entreat Queen Maeve relented and readied for the cold,

bringing with her the reason Guinn came he surmised.

Bundled in quilt upon quilt of the Mother's they arrived,

just as the Moon hid behind earth's shadow.

~

Dark, upon dark they made their way

down to Her chambers on stairs lit by torches.

Guinn a little tired, Maeve a little peeved,

but the mysterious guest actually seemed pleased.

The mother hearing their steps hurried across cold floor

just as they arrived, all three at her door.

Introductions and embraces were made in the midst

of the storm the Mother kept stewing and brewing.

All became quiet once the Mother beheld

The mysterious guest standing next to the Queen.

~

Graceful she was~ with

hair bobbing behind pointy ears in the shade of midnight

and emerald green eyes curtained by long lashes.

Practical yet elegant the Mother could see

was the fashion adorning the faery,

who happened to be,

the Daughter of January's Alder tree.

A black body woolen peeked out from underneath

an unusual, fitted waistcoat

of champagne satin in snowflake brocade,

with patterned flecks stitched in black silken thread,

clasped in the middle with one raven pin.

Long and slender sleeves drawing down to a point

stopping just shy of middle fingers

bedecked in dark smokey rings.

~

Breaking the spell her allure created,

the Mother heard this exquisite creature say,

"Tulla, Tulla Dannan's my name

I'm a faery of winter,

a maker of Snowflakes my fame."

"I, as your Mother, know of your work in the Queen's hollow.

She has tried year upon year to convince me to allow

your magick to fall outside of your realm.

I've dug in my heels, I can be stubborn you see.

But, I've had the planet to think of

to consider in all matters.

My fear is your flakes would disturb winter's muse,

to upend its stillness and make light of its peace."

~

Tulla, nodded her head understanding

the Mother's dilemma.

"My flakes are quiet and gentle.

They settle and nestle around nature's hidden places.

They protect and provide a blanket of white

71

to keep slumbering critters

deep into sleep

till spring's first light.

When soft and wet my flakes can be made

into playful statues and round snowy balls,

that please and ease from winter's icy dark.

I can help you and those in your lands

feel joy and hope in this cold winter's keep."

~

For the first time the Mother

heard from the source,

the value of light

kept on in the dark.

"Ahhh, yes I see!

Of course, Tulla Dannan we must welcome your flakes.

But, how does it work, what must you do,

to make flakes of snow rain down from above."

Tulla, smiled and winked at the Mother.

"I'm a faery, I know how to fool.

I couldn't have done it without you these years.

I wait till you stew and brew up a storm

Then, I blow icy breath as your bellows commence.

When you roar to let off steam

I turn anger, frustration and despair into flakes~ of peace."

The Mother so profoundly impressed

anointed on the spot,

Tulla Dannan, the Earth's

First Winter Faery, the Maker of Flakes.

~

As Tulla, and Queen Maeve turned to go,

the Mother happened to glance down at Tulla's feet and exclaimed,

"Aren't those my slippers I've missed

from your Queen's last visit."

"Why yes, my dear Mother," she laughed as she said,

"We counted on feet bare to the cold to finally change your mind

and hence nature's course."

As Tulla and Queen Maeve rode back to Marsh Hollow,

the Mother, feet still bare with an arm around Guinn watched from her window below.

Her view once clear now speckled in white

brought in the New Year.

The first ever covered in snow.

Made by the Mother's anointed,

Tulla, Tulla Dannan,

The Mother's Snowflake Faery.

That's how she's now known!

Close Your Eyes to Open the Third

A Grounding Exercise

Reader, instruct the stewards to hang their peace pendant around their neck and hold their Snowflake Obsidian in their hand.

Reader, recite after everyone is comfortable:

Breathe Deep,

draw in through the Crown

to connect self with spirit,

Exhale the World.

Breathe Deep,

draw in through the Brow

to receive second sight,

Exhale Outward Vision.

Breathe Deep,

draw in through the Throat

to speak your truth,

Exhale Self-doubt.

Breathe Deep,

draw in through the Heart

centering will to love,

Exhale Power's Misuse.

Breathe Deep,

draw in through the Solar Plexus

to restore connections with self and others,

Exhale Insecure Dependence.

Breathe Deep,

draw in through the Navel

to make love,

Exhale Societal Inhibitions.

Breathe Deep,

draw in through the Sacral

live long and healthy,

Exhale Dis-ease.

Reader, instruct the stewards to hold their stone in their lap resting above the sacral chakra.

Resume:

Breathe Deep,

again.

As you exhale,

feel the strong, silver cord

reach to the Mother,

deep in the Earth

to the center, her womb.

Planted within,

now safe and protected,

> *breathe once more,*
>
> *long breath out.*

Reader, the stewards may open their eyes briefly before we begin our guided story of *The Winter Traveler.* Instruct them to continue to hold the stone over their sacral chakra or slip it into a pocket.

The Winter Traveler

Our Guide for the story is Princess Periwinkle of the Crescent Moon.

Reader, recite as Princess Periwinkle of the Crescent Moon:

The traveler felt the weight of her heavy coat and boots, adjusting the pack slightly as she kept her eyes on the narrow path. Gone since morning, the journey was now her world once surrendering to the wintry hike in the woods. Alone, her breath eventually kept pace with her steps as her thoughts drifted, never dwelling long in one place. She was enjoying the simplicity of the day. Her senses attuned to nature as the hike took her deeper into the forest of Cavan Adair.

She stopped to rest, gazing far into nature's serenity. Snowfall overnight had cast the woods in crystalline stillness. Winter brown trees turned black as snow soaked into sleeping trunks. Beyond the path, snow drifts molded by rocks and fallen trees became heaping sculptures in white. But mostly, it was the tiny footprints that caught her eye, marveling at their gentle disturbance of the forest floor. The Sun came out briefly to turn the last layer of fallen flakes into a sheet of prisms. She watched as pastel bits of pearly essence danced back to the Sun. The forest was pristinely beautiful and cold.

All of a sudden, her senses seemed to converge on this singular point causing an acute awareness of the time of day and the lengthening shadows across the snowy floor. She remembered the dream and the Raven telling her to find MoonHaven before nightfall. After which time, the doorway to the underground sanctuary would be shut, locked until morning. The traveler didn't want to be left out in the cold.

She began to hurry in what she thought was the right direction. Before long she doubled back confused and almost lost. She took a couple of deep breaths, closed her eyes and envisioned the Raven. When she felt calm again she opened her eyes and was not surprised to see the vision perched on an Alder branch just above her head. A look of recognition passed between them. A silent agreement was reached to continue on together. The Raven was quite spectacular to watch. Jet black wings soared ahead, he looked back and soared on again. The raven never got too far out in front always, staying within the traveler's sight. She trusted this bird implicitly. As the day began to close, the Raven delivered the traveler to the very hill she imagined in the dream.

As she began the walk up the hill she caught the silhouette of a lone Alder tree and the figure of a man. The Raven, flying on ahead was now sitting on his shoulder enjoying a gentle smoothing of his feathers. There was obvious affection and respect between them~ the tree, the man and the Raven. "You made it," said he, "and just in time." The traveler was puzzled. "The Raven told me," the figure replied. "We have a long history that brought us here to MoonHaven, the Mother's slumberland. The Raven and I are Her guardians, the protectors of the Mother's keep."

"Allow me to introduce myself before we begin. I, am God Bran, a warrior of legend. I lost my immortality in a battle past. My spirit still leads through the Raven, offering protection to those desiring rest and peace." The traveler understood. She offered her name and they embraced. Her curiosity began to peak as she glanced over his shoulder for the entrance.

The Raven began poking at the bag hanging from the God's belt. Bran smiled and said, "There are two doors you must pass through to gain entrance to slumberland. The first door is through you. I need to ask, why did you come here?" "I desire peace, a break from this world," the traveler answered a bit wearily. As the words were spoken, the traveler felt a loosening from within and then a gentle click. A disconnect with the outer world had begun. "Ahh, well done!" Bran was pleased as he opened the bag and held it out to the traveler. "Put your hand inside and draw out one stone and one pendant. Relax, they will choose you." She reached inside and without hesitation pulled out one of each. The stone was Snowflake Obsidian. The second gift was a pendant of peace strung with sinewy black cord. Both lovely! The traveler was a little startled to feel a warm current run through her body triggering a tickling and pleasing sensation as the energy flowed then, stopped just below her navel.

Bran waited until the circuit made its connection and then told her to slip the stone into a pocket to keep herself intact throughout the process of drawing down to the Mother. Bran instructed her to place the necklace over her head and step up to the knot in the middle of the tree. A symbol of peace the same size and dimension as her pendant was seared into the knot's center. Without hesitation, the traveler fit her symbol into the knot's, unraveling at once this outer and inner door to peace. She glanced back at Bran and the Raven just as they faded into the dark, Moonless sky. She quickly thanked them for their help and heard Bran say, "Have a good rest." as she moved through the tree. Her body less dense felt a pulsing and pulling inward. Her pack coming with her required a hard yank at the end.

Once through, her second sight quickly came into focus aided by the third. The inside of the tree was an immense towering trunk. Smokey glass lanterns suspended from sturdy vines emanated grounding waves of light as they gently swayed in the whistling night breeze. Burrowed windows descended in a spiral pattern down circular walls shaped by the inner bark of the tree. Their onyx casements bounced light around the entryway and beyond. The traveler walked out of the foyer and stopped. There were eight earthen paths set in the pattern of a Pa-Kua, an ancient Chinese symbol of protection leading to enormous entwined Alder roots in the center. Instinctively, she walked to the path located in the back and to the right where she noticed a sign with the word K'un hanging on the bark wall.

Footsteps from the root closest to her caused her to turn. Up from below the guide arrived to welcome the traveler introducing herself as Tulla, Tulla Dannan. The traveler couldn't help but smile and was further mesmerized by the faery while she listened to the whole story about the Mother's snowflakes. Tulla told the traveler that after being properly anointed she was promoted to Guide of MoonHaven. And yes, this job is in addition to flake making which she still enjoys. In fact, flakes began to fall as soon as she began telling the Mother's tale. As Tulla paused to observe her work, the traveler noticed the faery's snowflake wings begin to melt. Startled, the traveler caught her breath. Tulla started giggling and said, "Oh, no worries, my wings change with every snowfall. It's been happening ever since that bit of business over the Mother's slippers."

"They are awfully pretty," the traveler remarked. And indeed they were being a gift from Neptune to the Mother. They were satin dance slippers in a deep shade of iridescent sea foam. When Tulla turned towards the closet, the traveler noticed the whimsical touch of a small mermaid's tail waving tiny beads of Malachite and black Pearls. Ahh, no wonder the Mother

missed them so much. As they readied to go Tulla said, "We can put your pack here in the closet, you won't be needing it. Better keep your coat and boots on though till you get used to the stairs and we get down to where its warmer." Until now, the traveler hadn't thought much about where they were going exactly, or how. The dream only took her as far as the outer entrance. The Mother's Snowflake Faery sensed this and held out her hand. They stepped together onto the earthen path towards the root of Tulla's arrival. Tulla commenting as they walked along that every root extends down from this base to the mother's slumberland known to some as her womb, or her cauldron.

As they neared the center, stairs carved into the root became visible. The first step felt a little rough from the inlay of amber. Tulla babbled intentionally to ease the traveler's tension with the long descent. "The resin keeps travelers from slipping and helps dial their auric fields to a positive frequency. The railings are hinged in lead, a gift from Capricorn to keep you and the stairs safe. The Mother thinks it's important that by the time you sleep you've released the fearful hold the outside world has upon you. There's a couple of other things along the way to help with that," Tulla said reassuringly.

At some point, the Traveler noticed that the roots were no longer nestled in dirt. There was no more soil around them. They were now entirely below ground. Animal-like sconces came to life as they circled past them on the trunk's walls providing earthy illumination. Sage torches warmed the body and cleared the head as they slowly spiraled down the root stairs. And, though they were underground, the windows somehow still looked outside. "It's a trick of the third eye," Tulla said. Feeling a little flushed, the traveler took off her coat which Tulla graciously held for her. As they journeyed further, they began an easy and comfortable bantering back and forth. The traveler wasn't always sure if the tales Tulla told were real or faery. But, they served to put the traveler at ease, lighten her step and release the world above.

Around the time the traveler noticed a shift in the air, Tulla announced they were almost there. This pronouncement was met with part excitement and a little fear, but mostly a sense of ease. The exercise, faery conversation and the magick of slumberland was working. The traveler arrived feeling safe and sleepy.

What she noticed first was the floor. The roots had spanned out across the expanse of the space creating a smooth slightly wavy floor resembling the soft contours of a womb. A bed of leaves covered the natural wood warming and cushioning their tired feet. In the center of the room was a natural hollow beginning about 20 feet above the floor where the roots pulled apart to spread across the room. The effect created a high, open enclave sheltered by the separated roots, but not enclosed by them. Nestled within sat the Mother's cauldron, fired from all types of timber below. An herbal brew was filling the chamber with the soft, gentle aroma of minty chamomile.

Tending the cauldron was Morrigan, The Raven Goddess of the Shadow Side of the Moon. She was a tall beauty with long auburn tresses, dressed in a silk sheath a shade darker than her hair, and a black robe trimmed in spun gold. A wreath of Alder twigs woven with baby's breath, pinecones and tiny acorns encircled her head. The traveler noticed the Goddess wore a crescent necklace of red jasper low, below the navel. "Welcome," she said kindly, "The Raven told me of your arrival. I am Morrigan, the Innkeeper of MoonHaven." After the introduction, the traveler curtsied to the Goddess thinking that was probably proper.

A question that had been forming since she entered the underground sanctuary became clear and the traveler inquired of Morrigan, "What is this place?" The traveler became increasingly more animated as she went on. "I find it so unusual. Everything is out of proportion yet, strangely it makes sense. It's majestic and deliciously sumptuous, but earthy and homey as well. And, it makes me feel tingly and restful at the same time. I absolutely love it here," she sighed out of breath. Morrigan and Tulla laughed. Well, Tulla replied, "It was once the Olde Dannan Faery Palace. It's too long of a story to tell now, but let me just say that the slipper business was not the first time we Dannan's have had a contest of wills with the Mother." The traveler let it drop but did wonder if the Mother acquired the Palace before or after she lost her pretty slippers.

Morrigan suggested the traveler take a moment to get her bearings before going to her room. What she became aware of more than anything else was how centered she felt. The journey down with Tulla, the incense and camaraderie here in the womb made her feel indescribably tranquil, at peace with herself. She turned to Morrigan and said, "I'm ready, you can show me to my room." Morrigan turned to the cauldron and said, "Let me get a couple of mugs for you two. This should help you rest." Morrigan embraced the traveler, handed her a mug and sent her off with Tulla to get settled. Morrigan, the Raven Goddess, then turned and said, "Here you go silent traveler I brewed this mug for you as well."

Reader, resume as Morrigan, the Raven Goddess:

"I do see you, you know. I'm here for you too. Come with me as I show you to your room. See how every room is directly off from the Mother's chamber, her womb? And, how each door frame is trimmed in onyx to keep you and other travelers safe as you sleep? Take my hand, I'll tell you about the rest inside. This room has a smoky quartz lamp for light and meditation, a wardrobe with a comfy gown to change into, pen and paper and a built in cabinet to store worrisome troubles. The bed is hollowed Oak, one of the strongest and most protective of woods and I only use high end thread for the bedding to ensure its softness. The cauldron is kept burning at all times, but there is a thick throw my sister made last Yule on the bed if you get cold. You can watch Tulla's snowfall through the skylight or close the shade, the pull is on the wall by the bed. I think that's about it. Take some time to settle in, change, store your troubles. When you're ready, I'll be back to tuck you in."

Reader, allow a couple of minutes of silence for the silent travelers to settle in.

Resume as Morrigan, the Raven Goddess:

"Time to lie down. I'll cover you up. Here's a little lullaby to help you~ Drift to Sleep."

Drift to Sleep

Drift to sleep,

sleep to drift

away from noise,

the hustle of streets.

Drift to sleep,

sleep to unravel

the knot tied to inner peace.

Drift to sleep,

sleep out stress

of life's hurried pace.

Rest in the Mother's Slumberland.

Drift to sleep,

sleep to drift

loved and safe within Her womb,

drift with your soul in timeless peace.

Reader, after a few moments invite the stewards to return to the room and write down their slumberland experience. And, for those who would like to do so, share with the group.

Open the Circle ~

After the feast, open the circle expressing thanks for our storytellers and guides ~

Mother Earth

Father Sky

the Four Directions

Princess Periwinkle of the Crescent Moon

Griffin Guinn

Queen Maeve

The Raven

God Bran

Morrigan, the Raven Goddess

and,

Tulla, Tulla Dannan

After the Ritual

Put your Snowflake Obsidian and written experience inside your winter slumberland and place it in the Love & Relationship Bagua of the home or room for the rest of the season. When you feel the need to *Drift to Sleep, Sleep to Drift,* place the necklace over your neck and rest in MoonHaven for awhile.

All is Well in the Stillness of Her Womb

~ Blessed Be ~

Chapter 6

K'AN BAGUA

#2

IMBOLC

AQUARIUS

February

Welcome Your Bliss

February's Sensual Nature

We begin to lose hope in February that nature's deep freeze will ever cease. Even those who enjoy the season tend to be over winter's mood. It becomes harder to muster up any enthusiasm for the powdered dusting of snow, or more quiet nights at home. Once this disquieting realization surfaces, we still must face a few more weeks before any visible signs of spring emerge. The Great Mother in her wisdom and perhaps because she too is tired of the cold, offers her stewards a chance to dwell within winter's final month with one foot planted squarely in February and the other pointing slightly off towards spring. As such, February is a bit of a seasonal crossroads. Our efforts to entice the Sun back to us become more earnest as the spell of winter begins to thaw.

To remain present in February, we must resolve to see winter through. It helps to look for what we may have missed in our hurry to be done with it. For instance, upon closer examination the natural world actually exists in more than one shade of dark. There is surprising variation in color, even though, winter's vegetation blends in with the Mother's dark earth. A slow walk in a ravine reveals two aspects of the Mother's subtle shading: tree trunks that change from milk to dark chocolate after a snowfall, and the caramel and mocha-dyed groundcover. When the light wheat color of winter grass mixes with this cyclical dye, it forms a pale peach crust over the earth, warming winter's appearance just a little.

Water is one of the more fascinating elements to observe in winter. The Mother's chameleon transforms its texture and color as the temperature drops to freezing. In descending order, water can begin as cold rain, turn to pelting sleet, blowing snow and end with a thick layer of caked ice. As the mercury falls altering water's form, so does our reaction to its new shape especially, when it freezes. Ice is a visceral encounter with the Mother. Her chilly reception seems to trigger either an artistic impulse or a survival stance. Depending on our perspective, we view this consequence of winter as either chiseled beauty or treachery in the making.

Regardless of our natural inclination towards this often brutal time of the year, winter does afford us an opportunity to gaze at the world differently through the Mother's picture window paned in seasonal black, milky white, or crystalline ice. When ice stops just short of destruction it stills the earth into a silken, translucent dream state. Winter's ink creates serene natural ornamentation that distorts, bends and softens the look of reality offering a mental escape from the winter doldrums. After a storm is an ideal time to peer into this altered world. Look for the perfectly round see-through droplets that hang frozen by the hundreds along tiny branches. Their simple execution rivals human construction as only the Mother can. Sometime this month, brave a winter walk and experience the power of cold in the breathtaking change of a waterfall frozen in midair and marvel at the cascade of ribboned ice.

Sometimes, our winter amusement comes from joining forces with nature to create athletic and artistic outlets. Winter sports and art reminds, suggests and invites us to live outside our familiar dimension if even for just awhile, until, the ice melts. These co-designed endeavors with nature captivate us differently. Our otherwise tangible experience with natural elements is surreally twisted forcing us to look at life beyond its natural borders. We need outlets to push us past unquestioned conformity especially in the season that can restrict our activity to the point of confinement. Snowboarding and skiing seem to defy our body's understanding of natural laws and showcase our instinct to push past them. Those who like to skate may take a break from indoor rinks and enjoy the discovery of a pond frozen after its still waters succumbed to prolonged frigid air. Any skating venue offers the graceful exhilaration of metal on ice. However, the athletic artistry required and mastery of balance and poise necessary to fly on skates feels more etheric in a natural environment. Some artisans use ice to sculpt otherworld possibilities. An ice sculpture's delicate sheen belies its solidity as it glistens in momentary grandeur. These athletic feats and works of winter art subtly display the alchemy of bliss: know your joy, stay present, follow nature's synchronicity.

As we brave the outdoors for some fun after feeling confined and cooped up inside, there is nothing better to warm us up again than a bowl of chowder. Chowder is the Mother's soup. It is deliciously thick with butter, whipping cream and cheese. Seasoned with celery, carrots, potatoes and onions, it's healthy as well. Chili is our other favorite dish this time of the year. Chili in the winter is like barbecue in the summer. There is stiff competition for the best and spiciest recipe. All kinds of things get thrown into chili besides tomatoes and peppers and most contest enthusiasts aren't likely to spill the beans.

A Visit to the Wise Hazel Tree

After living through a season that strips us bare naked to our core leaving us in

shivers, it's a good time to do things that we love, light the fire within and entice

winter's thaw. Like us, the Wise Hazel Tree stamps one root and then another to stir

up her internal embers. As night falls, the Tree and steward huddle together around

the fire ringed with hot glowing candles recounting stories of joy, mischief and

glee. As their laughter dies down the Tree places something in the steward's hand.

The steward asks," What's this?" The Tree smiles and says, "wait and see!"

Branches of February's Wise Hazel Tree

Imbolc~ Candlemas

K'an~ Career Bagua

Vibration of 2

Sun in Aquarius

By the end of the month, the icy grip of winter begins to melt thanks to the spiritual advances of a certain red headed Goddess. Our universal need to see the greening of the earth is so great that we devote the first three days of February to the worship of this Irish Fire Goddess by the name of Brigid. St. Brigid's Day on the first and the Feast Day of St. Blaize on the third are the Christian and French versions respectively of Imbolc, a pagan holy day celebrated on the second. The holiday is also known as Candlemas. Traditionally, candles galore were lit on this holy day to tempt the Sun back home. The Great Mother in the maiden dress of Brigid begins winter's thaw by warming the earth with her hot breath, perhaps, in anticipation of the awaited consummation with her lover at Beltane. Brigid is a powerful Goddess honored for her protective devotion to the Mother's newborns. Still beloved today, Brigid remains a symbol for hope, birth and growth. New, artistic, or practical ideas, as well as those for global good, may be lit by her flame to blaze in youthful abandon, or controlled bursts depending upon the fire needed to fan our desires.

As the earth begins to wake from its deep sleep, so do our dreams of bliss. Our purpose this month is to discover these seedlings of bliss for planting and nurturing during the growing season. This spiritual intent may seem like a tall order but why not seek this tantalizing and illusive emotional state? Bliss is within our repertoire of positive emotions. It is natural and reasonable to desire this exquisite sensation. Once encountered, we're not likely to forget the piercing ray of happiness that races up through our center before bursting out from all sides leaving us achingly alive and craving more. Bliss is possible. It is the result of right timing, the turn of the head towards something: a person, an idea, a vocation, a moment that connects us with a core purpose. It may seem happenstance, but in reality it is a synchronous moment, the convergence of the known and unknown around a spiritual end. The direct connection is so immediate, so powerful, that we are left shaken. Once experienced we long to reawaken this feeling of unabashed rapture. Surely, it is within our spiritual makeup to increase the frequency of these moments.

Our infrequent encounters with bliss should not be interpreted as some innate inability, but rather our unfamiliarity with its source, the Mother and our underuse of a spiritual tool, our intuition. Bliss comes from a steady, resolute reliance on our innate intuition. We are born knowing on a deep spiritual level what we hope to accomplish in this life. Listening to our intuition gives rise to these intentions. Bliss signals the human self that we have happened upon a circumstance that directly connects to a core purpose. The best judge of whether an experience is true bliss or not is if we love what we are doing in that moment. If time warps in our favor and we feel gloriously in command while doing something that is joyful and seemingly effortless, then we are likely in the throes of bliss. If we are fortunate enough to discover something that sustains bliss over time, then we experience a continuous warm current of contentment much like a cat's purr. Perhaps, the reality of blissful existence includes both brief moments of electric happiness and extended periods of contentment. The difference may be contingent upon our skill, receptivity and the circumstances relevant to a core purpose. With most things in life, the more we practice, the better we get. There is no reason to think welcoming bliss would be any different.

The first step is willingness, giving ourselves permission to pursue a dream. Permission is key to unlocking the gates of intuition which gradually open the more we show up to receive the information. Initially, we may not always recognize our intuition as such. Experience helps us discern the difference in timbre between our human and intuitive voice. Experience helps develop trust in our intuitive voice to not lead us astray. This trust and discernment can actually highlight those areas of personal growth getting in the way of who we really are. At times, this results in our intuition leading us somewhere beyond the familiar because we haven't been living the life of our true self. The principle, 'To thine own self be true' is a grounding philosophy for personal growth and one we can bank on.

Presently, the principle carries too little cultural currency because we haven't clarified the difference between self evolvement and self involvement. Our true self is part of what we refer to as 'all there is'. Genuine personal evolvement occurs when our actions begin from this enlightened center. When our thoughts and deeds strike the true chord within, the reverberating waves of pure energy we experience throughout our being is bliss. This celestial bliss extends outward uniting us with the rest of the world for our highest good. Self involvement however, may be described as action that begins from our experience with the external world. The flow runs backward from the outside to the inside. The chord that's struck within is resoundingly dissonant and distinctly human. It's not bad per say, but off the mark and unfulfilling. The risk we run is perpetual isolation from our true self and disconnection from the rest of the world. To live beyond a lackluster, albeit comfortable existence, requires courageous fortitude. Hopefully, if seen as a choice and given the tools, most of us would choose a life of evolvement over one of self involvement. It certainly is a choice the planet is asking us to make. The ancient traditions available to us this month carry a heavy responsibility to help us reach down and bring our bliss to the surface.

Feng Shui can help us fathom the watery depths of our being to unlock our bliss through activation of the most mysterious of the Baguas, K'an. Known as the career Bagua in the western world, this Bagua's energy encourages this dive into internal waters and a leap of faith into unseen territory. To embark on this endeavor, we must trust in the reward of newfound joy and purpose. We must also assume that self discovery usually reveals what we desire and that which is getting in the way. Our desires and problems may both surface from the inner work this month that we will set in motion on the second of the month, the holy day of Imbolc. Centering the work within the watery depths of the K'an Bagua will activate the energy to help us welcome our deepest wish.

While the tradition of Imbolc gently warms the earth in readiness for spring planting, the Goddesses of love inspire our joyful seedlings. Februa, the namesake of the month February is a Goddess of passion and new beginnings. Be rest assured that she is doing her part to pacify our restless spirits while she gently stirs the natural world out of its restful sleep. Brigid's red hair reflects her more bold enticement of spring. Other familiar helpers this month in all things sensually arousing are Cupid and Goddess Venus. These romantic figures are generally thought of in terms of union with a lover on Valentine's Day. This month we call upon their powers and those of Brigid's to help us unite with the most sacred part of ourselves.

Keeping company with these impassioned, mythic beings is God Uranus, the first ruler of the universe. Dreams inspired under his watch stand a good chance of breaking free from our self-imposed manacles of conformity and mediocrity. Uranus, known as the planet of change, also helps explain Aquarius's audacious nature. Advocates of a life extraordinaire will find favor under this celestial influence. We couldn't ask for a better sign than Aquarius, the dreamer, to aid us on our quest. This Sun kissed sign dwells among the stars preferring an unconventional existence rich in idealistic pursuits. A futurist at heart, this sign propels individuals and nations towards the 'Age of Aquarius' which is our next stage of evolvement. So as we dream on a personal level it is also a time to dream on a global one, to identify hopes and wishes for our home, Mother Earth.

Complementing our highly spiritual intent this month is Amethyst, February's birthstone. Amethyst is a crystal whose beauty is best appreciated in its geode form. It is a highly attuned stone with a clear purple color that reflects its deep spiritual nature. There doesn't seem to be anything Amethyst can't be of assistance with. The stone has the remarkable ability to calm, center, transmute, uplift, protect, unblock and inspire. The synergy between Amethyst and Aquarius can set us on a visionary path. Together, they can help turn our life away from the mundane and towards our highest good. The manifestation power of the stone helps bring our Aquarian influenced dreams to fruition.

The ancient traditions thus far provoke and inspire us to reach for something beyond the familiar. We're being asked to risk what is known in exchange for what up until now has been illusive, our bliss. What sparks our ultimate discovery of bliss is the alchemy of convergence between intuition and synchronicity. February's numerological significance relates specifically to this phenomenon. Number two's attributes of harmony and rhythm are necessary ingredients for being in the flow, in the moment and living in the present. These terms speak to our instinctive ability to tap into our unique individual rhythm, which remember is part of 'all there is'. Living in rhythm sets the stage for the right dancers and musicians to synchronously converge. It is in these moments when we have the opportunity to step aside and allow bliss to choreograph the rest of our dance.

Prepare for February's Ritual

If possible, perform the ritual towards the end of the

month to allow time to discover your bliss.

~ Seasonings for the Wise Hazel Tree's February Brew ~

For the Ritual Altar~

An Altar Cloth

A Skeleton Key

A Bowl of Charged Water

A Purple Candle for Mother Earth and God Uranus

A Smudge Stick of Sage

A Bowl to Withstand the Fire's Flames

Stone of Amethyst for February's Intent

To Stand Next to a Symbol of Spirit

A Bliss Decree and List of Barriers

A Brigid Doll

Hearts and Cupids for Merriment

Candles to Scatter on the Altar

A Basket of Pinecones and Bits of Nature Gathered While Out and About

Chocolate Dipped Strawberries and Earl Grey Tea

Your Wand Made From a Stick

Tasks Before the Ritual

1. While out walking or when in the car, look for interesting snow and ice formations.

2. Either make or purchase locally made candles for the altar.

3. Select a doll (preferably with natural fibers) to symbolize Goddess Brigid.

4. Get outside and have some fun!!

5. Discover your bliss beginning February 2nd, Imbolc's holy day. In the Career~ K'an Bagua of the home or space, place a purple votive candle. Each morning prior to the ritual, light the candle, hold the skeleton key in your hand and recite this affirmation~

True Self

True self reveal to me

all of my heart's desire.

Speak to me through butterfly inklings

all that will make me flutter.

True self present to me

all of my mind's proposals.

Speak to me through everyday visions

all that is hidden, unknown.

True self bare to me

all of my physical longings.

Speak to me through sensual delights

whatever enlivens my soul.

True self I make this pledge

to accept all signs and clues,

in the manner and form they appear,

in trust and gratitude.

True self

once shown my bliss,

help me see it as such

and bravely take the next step.

Take your skeleton key with you and go about your day with expectant trust that your true self will reveal your bliss. If you are led to follow up on a hunch, do so. Otherwise take note of the revelations in whatever form they may arise.

6.   The night before the ritual sit down in the career Bagua, light the candle, and make two lists on separate pieces of paper~ one for bliss and one for barriers. Be as clear as you can be without forcing it. Keep your lists in the Bagua until the ritual.

7.   On Valentine's Day treat yourself and loved ones to a simple expression of your devotion.

8.   Attach a bliss charm to the wand.

<u>The Day of the Ritual</u>

Prepare the Ritual Feast~

Chocolate again? You can never have too much! The strawberries

add a little color to winter's look and may entice the Sun to return

a little sooner. Use your charged water to brew the tea.

Placement of the Altar~

Lay the altar cloth on the table

For the Four Directions~

Wand in the East

Sage and Burning Bowl in the South

Tea and Chocolate Dipped Strawberries in the West

Basket of Pinecones and Bits of Nature in the North

In the center of the altar place the purple candle for Mother Earth and God Uranus

Near the purple candle arrange the symbol for spirit and

Amethyst, set the Brigid doll before the candle

Place the skeleton key and papers near the burning bowl

Set the bowl of charged water in the West

Scatter the altar with candles, hearts and cupids for your merriment

Time to Smudge~

Cast the Circle~

Invite the Directions~

Reader:

Welcome Direction of East, Spirit of the Unknown. Throw open the door to my future.

Stand down the tremors of fear. Help me walk through this reality and into the next.

Welcome Direction of South, Spirit of Brigid, Breath of spring. Ignite the flame of

my heart's desire. Turn inklings into kindling, sparks into embers, fire into blaze.

Welcome Direction of West, Spirit of Perseverance. Fill me with courage,

the will to complete that which began on Brigid's day. Stamina, Fortitude,

and Power to Sustain, as leader of my destiny, I do so claim.

(Bite into the chocolate dipped strawberry and wash down with a bit of tea.)

Welcome Direction of North, Spirit of Winter. Rejoicing and rest was time well spent, safe and warm in the Mother's keep. Refreshed, rejuvenated, restored once more. I awake into tomorrow and dare to soar.

Welcome Mother Earth and God Uranus. It is February, the final month for snow, ice and bitter chill to fall from grey skies onto a dark earth. While grateful for the gift of renewal, I am anxious for the greening time to begin. So, it is with a sigh of relief that I bid winter adieu.

Light the purple candle.

The Year Brigid Hurried Spring

An Irish Ditty for Imbolc

by Duchess St. DatilWise

Reader:

Cupid stood with his hands on his hips and surveyed the village below.

Shaking his head, he turned to Brigid and asked,

"What just happened do you suppose?"

Hair flaming on end and close to the edge

Brigid rounded on Cupid and said,

"You're the one with the bag full of arrows

who insisted we needed them all."

"Yes," Cupid replied, "but that was after

looking into the well you cried,

How am I suppose to tell?

If only you'd waited like the Mother suggested

to discover your lover

at Ostara's gala.

There you will find your mate she said.

So, remember Maid Brigid, it was you who started this mess."

"I know it was me.

But it couldn't be helped.

I've started the green, but the ground isn't ready

to consummate my desires in seed.

Who could blame me?

And whom may I ask,

doesn't wish to be done

with winter's icy freeze?"

"You're right Brigid," Cupid said,

"I'm done with this season as well.

But what should we do to change what we've done

to the lads in the village below?"

With heads hung low, they muttered and puttered and circled around

each trying to undo what they sowed.

Until, Cupid looked up and wondered out loud,

"What exactly went into the potion?"

Brigid replied, while glancing away, "Only what the Duchess told me to use."

"Which was what precisely," Cupid asked?

"Rose petals, patchouli oil, orris root, and flakes of datil pepper," Brigid rattled off.

"Well," thought Cupid, "That shouldn't have done what it did."

"Are you sure you followed the recipe as directed?"

"Alright, alright, I may have adjusted it a bit!"

"What's a bit?" Cupid inquired of Brigid.

"I altered one of the ingredients to heat it up a smidge.

The potion called for a pinch of datil pepper but, I decided to add

two tablespoons instead," Brigid replied sheepishly.

"Oh, my goodness," exclaimed Cupid in exasperation!

"What, what did I do?" cried Brigid.

Cupid took a deep breath and informed her, "When I shot my

arrows dipped in potion into the hair of the village lads, it was suppose to reveal the intended One by turning his dark hair red."

As they looked down into the village

what they saw in His place~

were the lads of the town all sporting the same color of red.

They burst into laughter at the folly they created

forgetting for a moment what to do.

"Well, I suppose all will fade except my true love's hair.

Unless, it means...

I'm to bed all the lads with hair of red,"

teased Brigid, our Fiery Red Headed Goddess.

A Fresh New World

An Aquarian Meditation

Reader:

Water falls freezing into drops that hang side by side along branches.

Perfectly round the same size in diameter

hiding their difference inside.

Pick one from the line without giving it thought trusting the voice within.

Step up, close to the drop

and stare deep into the center.

While holding the view, relax your focus

allowing the edges to blur into fluid.

Feel yourself melt into the drop

safely suspended in air

with the weight of the world left behind in the present.

You're free to take in the future

and Begin a Fresh New World.

Created by you and blessed by the Mother the new world turns

slowly around for review.

What is it you see?

What is it you'd do?

If you ruled the world for a day?

Reader, invite the stewards to take some time and identify three or more changes they would make for a Fresh New World. Ask yourselves, if you could begin the world anew, how would it be different. Pass the bowl of charged water around the circle inviting the stewards to place their fingertips into the water while they share their changes for a new world. Reader, when everyone has taken a turn, place your fingertips in the water and recite:

Incantation for a Fresh New World

Aquarius, Water Bearer, Giver of Life

we offer these desires for a New World

and ask they be blessed by your idealism.

God Uranus, First Ruler of the Universe

we offer these hopes for a New World

and ask they be blessed by your leadership.

Goddess Februa, Protectress of New Beginnings

we offer these dreams for a New World

and ask they be blessed by your clarity.

Goddess Venus, Patroness of Love and Surrender

we offer these wishes for a New World

and ask they be blessed by your passion.

Great Mother, Fertile Womb of Nature

we offer these seeds for a New World

and trust they take root in Earth's Center.

Reader, place the bowl on the altar for the remainder of the ritual.

The Sacred Keepers

A Dedication to Bliss

Reader, instruct the stewards to place their bliss paper in their lap and recite as the steward:

Witch of the Mountain Trail,

Keeper of Intuitive Keys

in the month of Goddess Februa,

96

I hereby claim my Willingness

to pursue my rightful Bliss.

Reader as Witch of the Mountain Trail:

Steward of the Great Mother,

I have witnessed your

courage in the days past

to uncover your bliss.

I watched over you and encouraged your

dive into deep waters to give rise to your sweetest dreams.

You are fearless and pure of heart.

It is with honor and respect I grant you this key from the Mother.

Reader, place the keys in the stewards' hands and continue reciting as Witch of the Mountain Trail.

Steward, be aware~ two purposes hath the key,

one you have fulfilled.

Your Willingness to Release your Bliss unlocked your Intuition

which you heard and followed under Februa's care.

To move forward into the future you must also unlock your Power.

Take your key to the Shaman

the Mysteries of the Universe await their release.

Reader as steward:

Shaman Rising Phoenix,

Keeper of the Mysteries

in the Month of Goddess Februa,

I hereby claim my Power

to pursue my rightful Bliss.

Reader as Shaman Rising Phoenix:

Steward of the Great Mother,

I too have witnessed your

skill in the days past

to discern your bliss.

I watched over you and observed

your contemplation

of flutters, visions and sensations sparked by your true self.

You have a wise and curious mind.

It is with honor and respect I too bless this key.

Steward, I must ask one question before you go,

Is it your intention to move forward on your quest?

Reader as steward:

With all my heart and soul.

Reader resume as Shaman Rising Phoenix:

On the strength of your desire, your power is now released.

The Mysteries of the Universe are yours to use.

Three you've uncovered in deed.

One,

Willingness to dream

unlocks intuition,

the voice of the true self.

Two,

Understand the signs

however they appear

and follow synchronicity.

Three,

Clarify intention

to unlock personal power

and wisdom to guide the quest.

Take this key as you follow your dream, your steps will unlock the rest!

Reader invite the stewards to speak of their bliss before passing the list through the Spirit's flame. When everyone has done so, instruct the stewards to take their list of barriers and burn them one at a time in the Spirit's flame. Afterwards, recite this spell to transfix the energy:

Burn to Transfix

Lack, fear, doubt, fatigue

cauldron's tinder burn in flame.

Transfix this nite from

dark to light.

For in the morn

the myth foretells

a rise from ashes.

From pyre's fire

to blissful sky,

on brilliant feathers

futures soar on phoenix wings!

Reader, ask for a volunteer to take the bowl of water outside and pour it onto the ground around the base of a tree reciting the *Incantation for a Fresh New World*.

Open the Circle~

After the feast, open the circle bidding adieu to winter and expressing thanks to our guests~

Mother Earth

God Uranus

the Four Directions

Goddess Brigid

Goddess Februa

Goddess Venus

Cupid

Duchess St. DatilWise

Witch of the Mountain Trail

and Shaman Rising Phoenix

After the Ritual

In the Career Bagua of the home or room, lay your bliss decree underneath

the Amethyst stone to cultivate energy for spring planting.

All is Well in the Stillness of Her Womb

~ Blessed Be ~

All is Well Under Spring's Enchantment

Spring~ A Time To:

Implant Ideas ~ March

Tend the Soil ~ April

Discover the Divine Feminine ~ May

A Spring Poem and Essay

It's Spring!!!

Although, we mean no disrespect of winter's intent

come time for spring

we are beyond discontent

with the season's cold and stark merriment.

We seek green spells from Emerald shores

and tales of luck and Irish mirth,

to feel soft air, clear sky and mushy earth.

Oh Goddesses of Spring, be quick

and warm the frozen earth.

Sprouts, shoot forth in pastel birth,

pinks, purple and yellows first.

Playful petals awake from under

push and churn the crusty dirt.

Yawn and stretch and take a peak.

Dare to plop in daffodil bunches.

Brave the wind, the rain and thunder.

Return ye birds from winter havens,

perch and build in homes of past

made from scraps of this and that.

Oh Goddesses of Spring,

the wheel has turned the earth to green.

The time has come to plant our dreams.

It's Spring!!!

It is with a sense of awe and deep respect that we welcome the Mother's green equinox. The explosion of nature from underneath the earth's barren surface is the deliciously awaited surprise of spring. Watching the greening differs from following nature's turn from summer to fall. In autumn, we witness the gradual browning and dying of once familiar, vibrant life.

Spring is the reverse. This season we witness life growing out of silent death. Where fall is the close of life, spring is life beginning. The equinoxes represent the start and end of the life cycle. The solstices influence what we do in the in between.

An equinox turn is a dramatic bi-annual shift towards the opposite in weather and palette. The turn is bold at first but then slows down in pace taking hold and deepening only after the solstice it compliments. The spring equinox gently marks the lengthening of the day's light after the dark sleeping season. The pastel bloom of spring brings a sweet ache of anticipation. With each day a different tree, hedge, or garden plot pops in dotted color. The soft, mellow green of awakening earth enlivens the soul, uplifts the spirit and resurrects life. The greening of earth arouses human tenderness and compassion, inspiring a misty, soft spot for nature's newborns. Our hearts quicken with the touch and smell of new life: the yielding plumpness of tiny bodies, the feel of baby down and fuzz, and the clean smell of innocence. We applaud the courage of life growing instinctively towards the new light. And conversely worry when in nature's rush to bloom, buds misjudge the last frost.

It is with good reason that spring is for many the favored season. In spring, our moods are generally light with spontaneous eruptions of joy. We are bone grateful to be warm again. Our appreciation of lungs filled with fresh air is so great that we don't seem to notice or mind the quickening of life's pace. Mild and clear days begin to beckon new growth within and without. We use these words renew, return, reborn, rejuvenate to describe the season's internal and external impact. Each word reflects spring's opportunity to begin anew. In nature, life wants to repeat itself, sometimes, in exactly the same way. Sometimes it's in a new inspired version, as buds that shoot out of skinny cracks in sidewalks.

Spring affords us the chance to follow nature's lead and plant to sustain and plant to dream in arcing rainbow splendor. Spiritually, the greening of the earth coincides with sowing the seeds of our future under the divine guidance of the feminine. Ideas that germinated over winter are now ready for planting. The soil will require special tending to support our dreams. As our new adventures take root, we nurture, and watch as they shoot toward the sky. All is Well Under Spring's Enchantment.

Chapter 7

March

Implant Ideas

March's Sensual Nature

Mushy, Muddy March is a hybrid of sorts, neither winter nor spring with none of either season's best for show until, after the vernal equinox. Before then, March is spring's tease. A month long stretch of half-sleep right up to the point in which day seeks balance with night and we take our first yawn of fresh air. Our impatience with spring's slow coming is taken out on March. The new season is so close we can taste it causing our moods to be as mercurial as the month. It's the time of the year when we must hurry up and wait. To look outside in early March one couldn't tell the greening time had begun. Trees remain bare under overcast skies and skin stays cool to the touch.

Unpredictable weather rules this month. Rain and snow storms occur within a day of each other. Mother Nature adds wind to the mix to stir up the crunchy crust wiping clean her winter canvas in time for the courageous strokes of early spring. Sloshy brown slush soaks deep into a warming earth giving rise to the blooms of the crocus and tulip tree. These brave buds have been selected to represent the greening of the earth. Each year they throw caution to the wind and shout, *"Be done ye winter morns, tis time for Sun and longer days"* at once fulfilling their calling as the harbingers of spring. And then it happens, frosted over before their color spent, withered blossoms once again. But, oh what a glorious demise, to be the chosen blooms to mark winter's passing.

Our excitement builds toward the end of the month. All of nature rises to the shift in temperature. We witness the season's first mellow showing of green. Tight buds relax unfurling into blooms and leaves. Balmy air beckons the birds. Sweet songs greet our morning. This unassuming brush with early spring is in a word, divine.

The season sweeps our spirit and body towards the Sun. Our vista widens as we lift our head after months of watching our step. The Sun warms our skin. We begin to shed layers of clothing whether we should or not and like children refuse to wear coats outdoors. Socks stay put, but sometimes inside sandals instead of boots. Lightweight sweaters replace bulky weaves causing many to return to the gym to shed winter's insulation. We are eager to switch out of the deep, rich, earthy colors of fall and winter. We trade our warm and comfy mood for the exhilaratingly free and airy disposition of pastel. These pale shades of colored chalk suggest spring's soft, beguiling allure.

Gesturing in the Mother's season of whimsy, magick and charm are festive eggs and bowlers and bonnets sitting jauntily atop Leprechauns and bunnies. Easter egg hunts conjure up excitable fun in each fanciful stage from their painting and hiding to the squeals of their discovery. March festivities bring us together in jovial camaraderie. It is indeed a good time of the year to honor and celebrate our Celtic pagan roots and the virtuous egg. This revered symbol associated with Eostre, a Goddess of Spring also happens to be one of the most versatile foods around. Whether boiled, baked, or scrambled it dishes up nicely at any meal. It is the integrative staple in many culinary conceptions~ cakes, fried rice, breads, custards, sauces and nog. When cooked it fluffs, gels and gives rise to our creations. And, as we shall see it's a most delectable symbol of spring's whimsical divinity.

A Visit to the Wise Hazel Tree

Earlier the wind and rain had washed snow and muck from between the roots of the Wise Hazel Tree exposing a wee bit of green. The ground too wet and soggy for sitting, the steward stands next to the Tree smiling with an eye toward the horizon as the Sun sets a little later in the day. The smile turns curious when out of nowhere a hare steers a wheelbarrow full of eggs right past him and begins to hurriedly bury them one by one among the roots. Much pleased, the Wise Hazel Tree whispers softly to the hare, "Job well done Mother Sky Rabbit."

Branches of March's Wise Hazel Tree

Ostara~ Spring Equinox

Sun~ Wealth & Prosperity Bagua

Vibration of 3

Sun in Pisces

The Great Mother's brown, still earth turns a soft cheery green as winter melts into spring. Goronwy, the God of Dark whom we met at Mabon, makes ready at last to hand the ruling time over to his opposite at Ostara, the spring equinox. Balance between night and day is regained as God Lugh returns on tides turned by Neptune's staff. By the morrow, daylight will be restored and begin its sunny reign thus triggering the Mother's planting season. Hearts ignite as maidens and lads nurtured by the Sun mature in equal standing. Courtships begin their mating dance towards consummation at Beltane in May. Inward balance shifts as receptive yin opens to active yang awakening sleeping dreams. Signs of spring bless us once again.

In the spiritual realm, spring is the rebirth of the light. At Easter, Christians rejoice in the resurrection of the Sun God, Jesus. Pagans similarly honor the season's place in the cycle of life in their worship of Eostre, a Goddess of Spring and namesake of the Christian holiday. Both pagan and Christian traditions in their own way believe in the soul's eternal light through faith. Both traditions hold joyous festivities proclaiming the profound gratitude we share for this spiritual blessing.

Other female deities across many cultures are celebrated around Ostara including Isis, Persephone, Astarte, Athena and Aphrodite. These Goddesses of Spring known for their fertility enliven the earth awakening pastel shoots from underneath. They help us welcome newborns of every species ensuring the continuation of the life cycle. One Goddess in particular, Persephone has a special reason for the season's rejoicing. For she is also a Goddess of the land of the dead, spending half her time below the earth. Each spring she returns to the living and helps the Mother during the planting and growing seasons. When the underworld calls for her return, her commitment to purpose is not unlike Jesus who ascended to the otherworld to watch over us.

Interestingly, eggs and bunnies are entwined with the holiday of Easter yet, it is with Goddess Eostre not Jesus in whom they've enjoyed a longstanding association. Eostre is responsible for the delightful Easter bunny tradition. According to Edain McCoy, the hare, Eostre's totem secured her favor by bringing the Goddess merrily ornamented holy eggs. The heartfelt gesture so touched Eostre that she sent the hare across the world to deliver eggs bedecked in leaping cheer. The egg signifies the cycle of new beginnings and is the most enduring symbol of our pagan legacy and the renaissance of the Goddess. It sustains our trust in the Mother's turn of the wheel to light after dark and life after death. It is through our efforts to succeed that we implant our eggs into the Mother's earth enriching the soil and germinating our ideas into life.

The egg embodies our resilience and tenacity as human spirits to rise up out of adversity and claim a new day. History reveals we don't always learn from our mistakes but, herstory commands that we get up and try. Today, the karmic connection to the Easter egg hunt of old is a less known aspect of our contemporary tradition but is relevant to the month's spiritual theme of rebirth. The egg represents life as we make it. When we hunt for the egg, we are taking personal responsibility for going after our hopes and dreams, for life is not handed to us in the asking.

This leads us to an important matter in this season of spiritual grace. Up for discussion is the concept of atonement and the fundamental difference between pagan and Christian teachings on the subject. Simply put, spiritual creed places ultimate power for grace either in the hands of an external God or an indwelling one. Pondering the difference arises not from a desire to be divisive but to raise the point that religion underscores the circumstances in which personal responsibility is exercised and why. The direct connection to our belief in salvation elevates the subject's importance this month. In Karmic philosophy we reap what we sow for good or not. Redemption comes in correcting the wrong inflicted. Sometimes, after we experience that which we did to another. In Christian teachings, redemption comes in acceptance of Christ as our savior. Both paths encourage learning from our mistakes. Only one requires it to receive spiritual grace.

When we put off the reward of salvation until the afterlife, we miss opportunities to make amends and enhance our evolving spiritual nature in the present. Waiting diminishes the gift of at-one-ment with the God and Goddess here on earth. This is not to say that pagans are more righteous and responsible, or that Christians care little for the impact of their actions upon others. We all share in the best and worst of humanity regardless of our faith. It's doubtful that humans ever liked being on the hook for their transgressions. The emotional aftermath can be uncomfortable and all too often, a damning and shaming experience. As spiritual beings, we need to grow beyond the discomfort of failure by coming clean to those we've hurt and accepting the consequences of our actions. If we act on our remorse, it may be easier to do the right thing the next time. In this holy season when Divine Grace sets the soul free~ Embracing Personal Responsibility will help guide its course.

As we embark on the spiritual path of March, Pisces, our Sun kissed sign aids in our efforts to ably respond. The sign is associated with reincarnation, a synchronous connection to spring and life made anew. Pisces joins with the Goddesses of Spring to gently awaken our desires. This water sign is ruled by Neptune, the God of the Sea. Neptune is another zodiac dreamer and lives most comfortably within the mysteries of the spirit world. Pisceans have a softness of being, a tenderness like spring, an artist's soul. The sign's energy gravitates to the core of a matter gracefully side stepping appearances to discover the essence within our dreams.

Ostara's emphasis on the reproductive aspect of the life cycle makes it a decidedly more feminine holiday. Coincidentally, Moonstone, Pisces' companion is charged with receptive, feminine life giving energy. The stone's connection to the Moon enables us through intuition to unearth our desires. As we brush the dirt off, we shine up our dreams just in time to plant them in enriched soil. These efforts can be taxing. At the festival of Ostara, Pisces and Moonstone will offer their soothing and compassionate energy to the Mother's stewards, her dream walkers in spring's first month of planting.

The Wealth & Prosperity~ Sun Bagua was chosen for two reasons. The first is obvious, the other less so. This Bagua's power has the ability to harness energy to manifest abundance as defined by us. Ideas for our future that we have worked hard to discover and clarify will benefit from the 'Sun' energy. Piscean dreams need a little help to materialize as follow through is not this sign's strong suit. This Bagua also encourages the patient, conscientious materialization of abundance over time. This quality underscores the importance of fortitude, a quality worthy of development in and of itself.

As with many months, the spiritual theme is often a balance between serious undertakings and light-hearted festivities. This is true of March. Even though it may not look like it, spring has arrived and planting is serious business. We call upon Numerology, the final ancient tradition to help keep our spirits bright as we Implant Ideas. We are blessed throughout the month with 3's freedom of expression and joyful inspiration. We stand by 3's optimistic belief that Ostara's turn of the wheel will eventually dot the earth with sprinkles of green. We trust the turn will occur in time to nurture our dreams.

Prepare for March's Ritual

If possible, perform the ritual on or near the Spring Equinox.

~ Seasonings for the Wise Hazel Tree's March Brew ~

For the Ritual Altar~

An Altar Cloth

A Pale Green Candle for Goddess Ostara and God Neptune

A Smudge Stick of Sage

A Bowl to Withstand the Fire's Flames

Moonstone (preferably the Rainbow Blue variation) for March's Intent

To Stand Next to a Symbol of Spirit

Paper for Grace

A Basket Nest

A Small Branch with Hanging Eggs

An Eostre Doll

A List of New Year's Wishes, Blissful Dreams, Ideas for New Beginnings

A 'Luck of the Irish' Symbol

Scatter Bits of Nature Collected While Out and About

A Dish of Custard and a Cup of Mint Tea

Your Wand Made From a Stick

Tasks Before the Ritual

1. While out walking about look and listen for signs of spring.

2. On one of your walks, pick up a small slender branch that catches your fancy. Hang a few glass, wooden, or ceramic eggs off the branch and hang it decoratively in the Wealth & Prosperity Bagua of the home or space.

3. Make a basket nest with bits of raffia and ribbon.

4. Make or embellish the Goddess doll to honor Eostre.

5. Don't wear a coat one day when you probably should have.

6. Experience the lengthening of daylight. What do you notice? How does it impact your mood, the day and bedtime ritual?

7. The night before the ritual allow your heart and mind to ponder that which you are ready to forgive in yourself and others.

8. Replace impatient thoughts of Mercurial March with this affirmation~

Vestiges of Winter, I give you leave

and gladly welcome spring's cool breeze.

For trailing on the winds of March

is newfound life in pastel green.

9. Brush off your lists of wishes, bliss and dreams and write them as if they are already achieved.

10. Attach a charm of new beginnings to the wand.

<u>The Day of the Ritual</u>

Prepare the Ritual Feast ~

Custard made from farm fresh eggs is a nice soft touch for the festival of Ostara. Mint, the color of early spring, brewed in tea is a gentle compliment. Be sure to use your charged water to make the tea.

Placement of the Altar ~

Lay the altar cloth on the table

For the Four Directions~

Wand in the East

Sage and Burning Bowl in the South

Tea and Custard in the West

Basket Nest in the North

In the center of the altar place the pale green candle for Mother Earth and God Neptune

Near the green candle arrange the symbol for spirit and Moonstone

Set the Eostre doll before the candle

Put the paper for Grace next to the burning bowl

Place the list of New Year's wishes, blissful dreams, and ideas

for new beginnings inside the basket nest in the North

Scatter the altar with bits of nature and the 'luck of the Irish'

Hang the branch with eggs somewhere within the sacred space

Time to Smudge ~

Cast the Circle ~

Invite the Directions ~

Reader:

Welcome Direction of the East, Spirit of Soft Air. Spiral wisps swirl and twist around the Mother's roots. Wake up, wake up they sing and call to petals yellow and purple. Grab hold we'll spin you out for all to see~ Ostara's blessed crocus.

Welcome Direction of the South, Spirit of Newborns. Plump and rosy, fuzzy with down, wobbly bobbles of sweetness and love. Sleepy yawns, furry paws, huggable charms of wonder. Squirmy and restless, messiest of messes, caring not for time of day. Eyes meet eyes, hearts do swell, besotted forever after.

Welcome Direction of the West, Spirit of Sea Breeze. Neptune rises above the surf to check on Eostre's progress. His head and hands exposed to elements, his measure of spring's ascent. "Not yet," he grumbles. Then flicking and whipping his tail in descent he impatiently returns to sea.
(Take a sip of tea and scoop of custard.)

Welcome Direction of the North, Spirit of Good Fortune. Rainbows point to pots of gold every color showing the way. Paths unfold in the hunt for eggs and treasures from ancient past. Spirits of fortune guide our quests on land in sea and air. Keep us safe and true to our aim as we journey to claim our dreams.

Welcome Spring Goddesses of the Mother, Isis, Persephone, Astarte, Athena, Aphrodite, Eostre, Ostara and God Neptune. Stewards, Behold the power of the divine feminine. Command the rise of serpentine energy. Pledge this sacred nite to nurture Ideas Implanted deep within our Great Mother.
Light the pale green candle.

Rooney, the Leprechaun's Gift to Persephone

A Tale from the Olde Country

Conspired by the Mother and the Leprechaun, Rooney O'Neill

Reader:

In exasperation, Persephone cried out, "Oh my, oh my, I'm late. I

forgot to change the clock to move the day ahead! It's almost three

past noon and precious little time to make my rendezvous."

"Whew, he's here. Sooo sorry Mr. Robin to have kept you," apologized Persephone.

"I brought what you desire, a strand of mermy weed.

"Yes, it works above sea.

For once upon a dare, Neptune used the mermaid's weed

to protect his tail against the salty air.

Just weave the weed around the nest times three as mama sings the peeps a tune.

Once safe and sound,

you're sure to get a good night's sleep," explained Persephone

"You're welcome Mr. Robin, now if you please we have a leprechaun to catch

up under Chanterelle's canopy, near Molly's tree."

~

"Oh, how pretty," she purred.

"Do you hear the faintest tinkling of strings,

the muse of harps as we draw near?

Could that be you Rooney O'Neill?

Please say tis true, for I would stay forever in Chanterelle's

garden betwixt by the song I hear," begged Persephone.

"Ah, Persephone you make me blush.

I would keep you here, and risk the Mother's displeasure if I too did

not benefit from your gift of spring," flirted Mr. O'Neill.

"Why, Mr. O'Neill you are indeed a charming fellow. But,

the hour grows late, I must make my appeal.

On Ostara Eve as I made my ascent from below I was

feeling a little tired and not up to the task.

So, I called God Neptune, a friend from the past, who referred me

to you, the cobbler of shoes and maker of magical tools.

He told me of slippers you made for the Mother.

I thought perhaps, you would make me a pair but, only if it's no bother," she entreated!

"Well, well, well, so this is what I owe the honor of your visit

to make magical shoes for a Goddess of Spring.

It will take me till dawn to make what you're after.

But, don't be surprised if while you sleep the Mother and I conjure

up a better idea," replied a bemused Mr. O'Neill.

"Off with ye now Mr. Robin, back to your nest. Here Persephone dear, lie down and

take rest under the canopy of Chanterelle," commanded the mischievous leprechaun!

~

Persephone was lulled to sleep that nite by the gentlest of rain and the sweetest of lullabies.

In the morn, she awoke content, refreshed and enveloped in a plush purple cloak

made from the softest of wool and down and trimmed in fanciful feathers.

~

"Oh my goodness, how lovely," she purred.

"It is a gift to you from the Mothers of the Forest and me.

Mr. Robin inspired by the Mother as he flew home,

called out for remnants discarded in yesterday's shedding.

Around midnight the most boisterous of undertakings commenced.

I've not heard such clucking, hissing, mewing, and chirping ever in one place.

Over the course of the nite each feather, fiber and strand was imbued

with love and magic for your command," relayed a most delighted Mr. O'Neill.

"It's reversible, you see!

One side for light times the other for dark and the skin of the snake lines the in-between

to remind you when it's time to switch behind or ahead.

The cloak is graced in two shades of luscious: lavender

for spring and a royal hue when down under.

Two sides~ two purposes~ your life in full circle.

A spell of your making is charged in the spirals embossed on both

sides. Decide what's best to accomplish your calling,

what's needed in the land of the living and that of the dead," he proudly explained!

~

"Rooney O'Neill I am swept away by this gesture and bestow upon you and

the kindhearted forest a kiss and my blessing of eternal devotion.

As for the Land of the Living, this cloak will Spiral Rainbow

Mist upon each shade of green for six months hence.

When Walking Among the Spirit of the Dead, the spirals will Emit the Essence

of Pettigraine to rejuvenate, calm and uplift," conjured Persephone.

~

"So mote it be, Goddess Persephone," blessed Mr. O'Neill.

~

"I'm ever so grateful, Rooney O'Neill.

But, I must say I'm a little surprised

by your straightforward dealings.

This is so unlike Leprechaun legend."

"Well, Goddess Persephone you discovered the trick.

When you out charm a faery your problem is ours to

fix," replied Mr. O'Neill with a grand bow!

"Be off with you now the forest awaits the coming of spring.

But, if ever you need a wee bit of rest~

come, catch a nap up under the Canopy of Chanterelle~ near

Molly's tree," invited the Leprechaun, Rooney O'Neill.

Grace, Spirit's Ballet

A Poem for *Grace*

115

Reader:

Grace, Spirit's Ballet.

Love in motion, Elegance in form.

Dancing to music, Played on wings, Favored by hearts.

Poised in patience, Await the beat, Leap in faith.

Skyward beauty, Polished style, Soaring charm.

Misstep in landing, Music silenced, Movement stops.

Legs draw up in first position, Grace in Repose.

Dance renews, Soul changes note, Played by wings.

Grace, Spirit's Ballet.

Reader, allow the stewards the opportunity to write down those things for which they are ready to forgive in themselves and others and burn the list by spirit's candle. When the lists are burned recite this blessing:

Tides of Grace

Hard to Forgive

the swells of injustice.

Work to repair

the damaged shores.

Allow tempers ebb

for tides of grace.

The Story of Mother Sky Rabbit

As Remembered by Their Daughter, Emma

Reader:

"Gather round little ones, a tale needs a telling this Ostara Eve. Hurry now, that's good loves, scrunch up close, but do mind that fire. Everyone hush now so I may begin," cooed Emma. Once long ago, lived a wee one named Bunny Sky Rabbit. An odd sort of name for a distinctly different kind of bunny. From the very first day she could hop she was leaping off rocks and ledges and anything high insisting all the while, that she was Destined to Fly. Of course no one believed her. In fact, she was the bum of much teasing, even the Council of Angora couldn't help poking fun.

Every night before bed, Bunny Sky Rabbit would scotch tape feathers to her long ears to teach them how to feel the wind. Every morning she would begin her day with a leap from the tallest mound with her ears outstretched as far as far can go. Bunny Sky Rabbit was blessed with unusually long ears and as she got older her ear span grew to three feet on either side. Those who knew her then say she always landed with a whoop and a holler. And, the brave few she counted as friends remembered she never gave up, ever, ever, no matter the weather or how many burrow bullies greeted her leaps with sneers and jeers. She would just cock her head to one side, smooth out her ears and bound off to heights jumped by none other.

This did not go unnoticed. Some burrow folk with more open dispositions would occasionally wonder if perhaps they should start scotch taping their dreams to various parts of their bodies, which usually led to some pretty funny ideas.

Days and months went by, scotch tape turned to packing tape then, duct tape and finch feathers turned to meadowlarks and then, peacocks because Bunny Sky Rabbit's ears had grown so big they now reached five feet on either side. The word spread to other burrows and then more burrows, until most folks in and around these parts knew about the bunny who thought she was Destined to Fly. What wasn't told in the papers was the run on all manner of tape and the number of odd looking bunnies at bedtime.

Bunny Sky Rabbit just shy of full grown amused by her newfound popularity continued to leap off the highest ledges and bluffs every morn. Then, one early spring day after an especially daring leap, she landed at the feet of Eostre, a Goddess of Spring. She knew of this Goddess because of her kindness in growing colorful delectables in the burrow's gardens.

Bunny Sky Rabbit smoothed out her ears and smiled up at Eostre. The Goddess returned the smile with a scratch behind the bunny's ears pulling off a bit of packing tape as she said, "Good job Bunny Sky Rabbit." The bunny cocked her ears perplexed.

"When you were born," explained Eostre, "your mum prayed to the Mother and asked her to turn your long, long ears into a blessing instead of a curse, which she did. The Mother's blessing would fulfill a dream of your making if never, ever you gave up!" Upon hearing this, Bunny Sky Rabbit's ears popped out on either side ready for flight. Eostre laughed and told the bunny, "What the Mother didn't count on was your dream touching the hearts of so many. Because of your gift to lead, she has a job for you which may be fulfilled once a year."

"On Ostara Eve, from this point on Bunny Sky Rabbit you are to fly around the world and gather up dreams to be planted by me and my sisters, the Goddesses of Spring. Could this be your destiny?" The bunny nodded yes so passionately that her ears started to buzz and whir and with a bound and a leap she was flying, really flying. Eostre ran after the bunny and hurriedly threw her the basket as she shouted, "The Mother said I could change your name if you said yes. From this nite forward you are to be known as Mother Sky Rabbit, Friend of Eostre, Gatherer of Dreams."

"And, so little ones every Ostara Eve, be sure to write down your dreams and leave them in a basket on the doorstep for Mother Sky Rabbit to swoop and scoop them off in flight to the Goddesses of Spring," bid Emma!

Reader, invite the stewards to place their Wishes, Bliss and New Ideas into the basket nest commenting upon them if so desired. When everyone has done so, begin the incantation by circling the Hanging Branch of Eggs over the basket nest while reciting:

Incantation to Implant Ideas

Neptune,

God of the Sea

we invoke the power of yang, the divine masculine

on this nite of sacred fertility.

Impregnate

our dreams of new life

with your life giving waters.

~

Ostara, Isis, Persephone, Astarte, Athena, Aphrodite, and Eostre,

Goddesses of Spring

we invoke the power of yin, the divine feminine

on this nite of sacred fertility.

Implant

our dreams of new life

with your emerald enchantment.

~

Mother Earth, Father Sky

balanced divinity.

Protect and nurture

our dreams of new life

with your fertile soil and lengthening Sun.

Open the Circle~

After the nite's festivities are complete, open the circle

with gratitude for our Springtime guests~

Mother Earth

Father Sky

the Four Directions

God Neptune

Goddesses Ostara & Eostre

& Sisters of Spring~

Isis, Astarte, Athena, Aphrodite & Persephone

Rooney O'Neill & the Mothers of the Forest

and

Mother Sky Rabbit, Friend of Eostre, Gatherer of Dreams

and their daughter, Emma

<u>After the Ritual</u>

Place your basket nest of new beginnings on the doorstep overnight for a blessing

by Mother Sky Rabbit. The next day, plant your ideas into the soil underneath a

strong, sturdy tree. Leave your Moonstone in the Wealth & Prosperity Bagua of

the home or room. Slip it into your pocket if ever you need a ray of hope.

All is Well Under Spring's Enchantment

~ Blessed Be ~

Chapter 8

CHEN BAGUA

#4

EARTH DAY

ARIES

April

Tend the Soil

April's Sensual Nature

Sometimes, depending on where you live, March's spring tease rolls into April. Temperatures do rise, but only incrementally, fifty degrees will replace last month's forties. When the Mother strings a few days of high sixties in a row, we assume warmer weather is here to stay. Still wet and rainy, April is known for its showers, umbrellas and trendy galoshes. Coats are mostly gone as light jackets come out and socks are on and off throughout the day. It's a hard month for fashion. We end up dressing in an interesting bi-seasonal mix and match of fabrics, foot attire and sleeve lengths. Homes haven't made the switch either requiring the heat to remain on, especially at bedtime and in the morning.

We tend to hear spring before we see it. In early April, the migration of the songbirds back to us is the most evident sign of spring. If not for our feathered friends, we just might despair with the slow visual turn of the season. Their harmony reminds us that their absence was the cause of much of winter's stillness. During the month, we begin to notice the lone solo now joined by a full choir. Morning routines are graced with the sweet sound of their happy homecoming. Many a sonnet was inspired by the songbird's lyrical return on jubilant wings. Their twittery company provides us much needed reassurance that the greening of the land really is just a weekend away.

And, what a greening it becomes. Daffodils, one of the first flowers to bloom, enjoy their maiden presence. This spring favorite has the same fetching allure as an old time garden party of southern belles admiring each other's flouncy skirts. The coquettish daffodil loves to surprise by bursting upon lawns in giddy bunches, gracing the sloping line of a garden walk and revealing the steep incline of aging stone steps. This unabashed beauty opens our eyes to spring, as do young trees who seem to green up first, absorbing our delight while they can, knowing their older friends will soon capture our attention.

There's always a point in time when we throw caution to the wind and claim spring. The trigger could be the row of forsythia in bloom on the side of the house, the pots of pansies on front stoops, or the pink and white tree line of cherry blossoms and dogwood. Whenever it happens, be assured that even another frost can't dampen our spirits. It just feels so good to be outside. All season enthusiasts are joined by warm weather joggers. Shiny new bikes stored since Christmas are ridden by kids out front, under their parents' watchful eye. Cars, salty from winter's last storm, are washed in driveways with soapy buckets of water simply, because we can. We don't seem to mind chores so much if they take us outside for winter's toll must be dealt with to cultivate spring.

We join forces with the Mother to clear the path for new growth. Her thunderstorms and our rakes are the tools. By late morning, the songbird's concert is joined by the hum of yard work. We tend the soil enriching it with nutrients to support annuals and perennials. Spring blooms within us as well after brushing away the crusty sleep from our eyes. We begin to shore up our inner foundation ensuring our continued success and achievement of new endeavors.

A Visit to the Wise Hazel Tree

The steward takes a break from raking leaves around the roots of the Wise Hazel Tree. He takes care not to disturb the peeping posy of daffodils. He sits down spreading his legs out front and rests his back up against Her trunk. After awhile, he closes his eyes for a bit. A swish of tickling air stirs him awake almost upending the lunch placed upon his lap. A card reads~ For the Mother's Steward~ a simple salad of field greens with strawberries, nuts and feta cheese tossed in a light poppy seed dressing~ accompanied by the sandwich of the day, a crusty baguette filled with spring onion crème cheese, cucumber, tri-color peppers and sunflower seeds. Resting on his leg is a pint-size bottle of Belle's Sassafras Soda. Between bites he manages to ask the Tree to whom he should direct his gratitude.

She laughs and says, "Well steward, I believe you have just been treated to lunch by Mirabelle, the Songbird's Faery." Upon cleaning his plate, an invitation the size of a postage stamp comes crawling up his pant leg on the back of a teensy ant. To his delight he has been invited to a matinee performance at The Concert Hall of the Cardinals on April 22nd.

Branches of April's Wise Hazel Tree

Earth Day~ April 22nd

Chen~ Health & Family Bagua

Vibration of 4

Sun in Aries

Spring is the perfect season to honor earth, our home. The planting season renews our commitment to nurture the natural world. Its overpowering allure commands our appreciation as we are drawn outward by Spring's enchantment. We step outside to experience the greening of the land, listen to the songbirds' homecoming and breathe in the sweet essence of hyacinth. Each glorious breath allows us to more fully realize our connection to nature. The greater the intake of breath, the deeper our commitment becomes to care for the Great Mother. The founder of Earth Day, Senator Gaylord Nelson, rightly chose the season of spring to celebrate our earthly home.

Since 1970, Earth Day has served as a symbolic reminder of our responsibility as Her stewards. Senator Nelson is credited with helping Americans reappraise our fundamental connection to earth. He understood the reciprocal relationship we have with our planet. Nelson encouraged a civic response to this inherent reciprocity, recognizing our continued survival was dependent upon community action. The grassroots environmental movement begun over forty years ago has improved the quality of our water, land and air in part, through corporate incentives and penalties. Yesterday and today, community markets serve the movement in a dual capacity. Local markets are the heartbeat of grassroots efforts, educating us on the viability of sustainable living and advocating for its benefits. Organic grocers, many of whom are community-owned businesses, teach the value of reciprocity through their green commerce.

Efforts have intensified recently because our destructiveness is outpacing our commitment. We are finally recognizing the detrimental result of the Mother's outmatched attempts to accommodate our misuse. Our footprint is about to change. It is time to tend the Mother's soil in full consciousness of the impact neglect has upon the earth and us. Along with increased governmental attention to the planet, we are now seeing a civic response across mainstream America. Earth Day celebrations have the capacity to marshal increased personal commitment to the environmental movement, offering proof once again that monumental change begins and ends with each one of us. Momentum is growing. We are almost strong enough to influence on a larger scale the daily practice of living green and in season with the Great Mother.

This month we will honor the Mother's greatest gift, the earth's yielding suppleness. Her lithe spirit forms the basis of our earthly and human foundations creating a symbiotic relationship between us. Earth is sustained by light and water. Nutrients and the lack thereof affect nature, just as they affect humanity's inner soil, our foundation. The noblest of goals will wither in undernourished ground. What the Mother needs to support new growth in supple ground is a fitting question for us as well. What do we need to support our new beginnings?

First, we sweep away the crusty impediments from our soul. We rake the dirt and muck that clings to our inner soil. This clearing frees our inner foundation to receive goal affirming nutrients. The nutrients needed for a supple foundation are hope, passion, knowledge and perseverance. Our manifestations more closely resemble our desires when our foundation has been properly tended. Humans are magical beings imbued with powers of creation for good or not. The power to manifest is neutral, taking no stand on the correctness of our endeavors. Goals and dreams bloom from our foundation. Therefore, it behooves us to clean up our act and fertilize our inner soil with goal affirming nutrients.

Hope, the first nutrient, is more powerful than doubt and fear, even in moments of rattling thunder when it seems to disappear. Hope may get shaken into a corner, but it won't remain there. Hope will rise to the occasion and face down despair. That is its job. Hope is aided by optimism and trust. Trusting our inner wisdom is also connected to the belief that all will be well. Trust helps us accept outcomes that we have co-designed with our own divinity, even when the result is not quite what we expected. We may at least take comfort knowing there is a divine silver lining that we can discover.

Beginnings are often sparked by passion, the second nutrient. It is a delicious, fiery excitement we feel deep in our belly. Passion is a focused directive, that when heeded, leads us to experience our best selves. Our best self is our true self. Living life on our terms is a universal desire. Living true to ourselves is acting upon discovered interests and talents and exploring them to their fullest. Living our passion builds upon itself until it bursts outward thus enriching the soil and those around us with sunny zeal.

The third nutrient is knowledge. This knowing is gained on our own and with the help of others. Sometimes, it means rethinking a tried endeavor. Other times, it involves cultivating new ground. Regardless of the impetus, expanding our knowledge engages the soul and keeps us young at heart. There are many ways of knowing. Formal resources such as school, trainings and books may be necessary to prepare ourselves for serious dream making. Like-minded mentors are also available informally to help shore up our knowledge base and skills. A degree of anxiety usually accompanies learning. The other nutrients, hope and passion, can temper the stress of the learning curve. Trusted others are also helpful in calming the nerves and securing what we need to begin and succeed. 'The more the merrier' adage actually helps our manifestation efforts by sending a clear message to the universe that we are serious about this idea. Equally important, is the enjoyment derived from involving others in our pursuits. Enlisting our cohorts and YaYas make for more exuberant life endeavors.

Perseverance, the final ingredient, is also necessary to bring forth our desires into manifestation. In its own right, perseverance is the steely resolve to see something through. It becomes a holy sword when coated with hope, passion and knowledge and forged in divine fires. We carry the sword of perseverance within us to keep our head up, our back straight and our feet firmly planted on the path of our highest good. Because, life intervenes at the most inopportune times, daily responsibilities, emergencies and unexpected occurrences happen. Without our holy sword, the resolve we worked so hard to cultivate begins to melt. Part of the grand design may be for us to move past the unanticipated, proving to ourselves and the universe that we will succeed.

To bolster our commitment to self and the planet during the Mother's stormy season we will draw upon the corresponding ancient traditions beginning, with Feng Shui. Chen~ the Health & Family Bagua expects the sudden, unexplainable events of life. Rather than damning the occurrence, the I Ching suggests we flow with the disturbance. This frees the energy to form a decisive plan. Directing its course is not easily done but doable. Our sword of perseverance cuts through obstacles a little easier and quicker each time we weather a storm. Building a strong foundation to survive and thrive is the spiritual gift of April and this Bagua.

Aries, the first sign of the zodiac, brings an enormous zest for life and limitless possibilities. This Sun kissed sign is passion incarnate. Aries' energy is rash, impulsive and courageous under fire. Protected and guided by God Mars, the namesake of Aries' ruling planet, we are compelled to stir the embers of change. Our warrior zeal is called to correct the injustices of the world. This month's zodiac fills us with both hope and dynamic energy infusing our soil and the Mother's with the Sun itself.

There is one correctable caveat to this fiery astrological energy. Unchanneled passion can fizzle under Aries reign. With all its glorious attributes, it's a bit of a procrastinator and the initial fire may burn itself out. With the help of Aventurine, Aries companion stone and the vibration of the 4 we can keep the fire at a steady flame. Their tinder provides a constant ardor from beginning to end. Four's energy is loyal, service driven, practical and patient. The vibration revs up for endeavors requiring endurance. Point the four in the direction of our dreams and it will help us apply all that is needed to bring success. Aventurine also brings qualities of perseverance to April's ancient traditions. It is a solid stone good for environmental activities. The green variety is especially fitting for tending the soil to bring prosperity to the Great Mother and her stewards.

Prepare for April's Ritual

If possible, perform the ritual on Earth Day, April 22nd.

~ Seasonings for the Wise Hazel Tree's April Brew ~

For the Ritual Altar~

An Altar Cloth

A Turquoise Candle for Goddess Danu and God Thor

A Smudge Stick of Sage

A Bowl to Withstand the Fire's Flames

Green Aventurine for April's Intent

To Stand Next to a Symbol of Spirit

A Danu Doll

Lists~ Tend the Soil & New Green Habits

Vase of Fresh Flowers

A Lemon Poppy seed Muffin with Raspberry Tea

Your Wand Made From a Stick

Tasks Before the Ritual

1. One morn before dawn's light, wake up slowly to the songbird's carol.

2. Sit outside and watch a bird gather bits of this and that to build a nest. Stick around long enough to spot the nest.

3. While out walking about breathe in the scent of spring.

4. Pick a tree in your yard or neighborhood that is an early bloomer and watch it green over the month.

5. Select one wish you have identified over the past rituals or a new one and tend the Soil for its development. Consider the goal affirming nutrients~ What cultivation is needed~ Hope, passion, knowledge and, or perseverance? Make a list. Be as specific as possible.

6. To Tend the Mother's Soil think of one item for each of the following green habits you are willing to implement over the next 3 months~ Reduce, Reuse & Recycle. Make a list of your commitments.

7.   Make or embellish the doll to honor Goddess Danu.

8.   Select a charm that represents the nutrient you most need to cultivate your soil and attach it to the wand.

<u>The Day of the Ritual</u>

Prepare the Ritual Feast ~

Lemon Poppy seed muffins are light and springy and a favorite of

Mirabelle's. Depending on the temperature have a hot or cold drink

of raspberry tea. Use your charged water for the tea.

Placement of the Altar ~

Lay the altar cloth on the table

For the Four Directions~

Wand in the East

Sage and Burning Bowl in the South

Tea and Muffin in the West

Vase of Flowers in the North

In the center of the altar place the Turquoise candle for Goddess Danu and God Thor

Arrange the symbol for spirit and Aventurine near the Turquoise candle

Set the Danu doll before the candle

And, lay the Tend the Soil list next to her

Place the New Green Habits list beside the Vase of flowers

Scatter the altar with mementos of Mother's spring

Time to Center and Smudge ~

Cast the Circle ~

Invite the Directions ~

Reader:

Welcome Direction of East, Spirit of Song. Melodies in harmony

drift to earth carried on feathered air. Join in the song of joyful

homecoming. Float into spring caressed by songbird wings.

Welcome Direction of South, Spirit of Warming Currents. Insides bubble and burble in excitable brew. Steeped in Sun, stirred by the Mother and concocted by you. Ready? Keep steady, now lavish your dreams.

Welcome Direction of West, Spirit of Blossom Hearts. Layers upon layers folded over and over till the last touches center. Blessed by the Mother layers upon layers unfurl and uncurl till the last reveals you.
(Have a bite of muffin and sip of tea.)

Welcome Direction of North, Spirit of Majesty. Breathtaking splendor, glorious shores and the freshest of air~ these are desires of the Great Mother and all living things. Live Well in the Green!

Welcome Goddess Danu and God Thor, Spirits of Spring and Change. Bless our celebration of Mother Earth and the dreams of her stewards. Sustain us as we Tend the Soil to sustain you.
Light the turquoise candle.

The Songbird's Venue
Written by Mirabelle, the Songbird's Faery

Reader:

Climb up...very quietly to the songbird's venue.
Once, the nest of Dottie the squirrel
and three jittery youngins
now grown and off to parts unknown.
An abandoned nest is a treasure in the rough
for the new Concert Hall of the Cardinals.
Built in branches in the tallest of trees,
out on the thinnest of limbs,
for acoustics unfettered are better in wind.
Fastened to bark with ruby studded string
keep concert goers aloft

Carolann Gregoire, MSW

and royal feathers unruffled.

Enter from the back as the grandest of views

features the creek down below

where the water streams by in musical backup

and the redbuds burst in time to the beat.

Duck through the door in the shape of a diamond,

the color of flame on the Cardinal's red breast.

Take to the center, down front to the seat

draped in gold tulle for Mirabelle's guest.

Look up before the concert begins

watch birds of Walhalla come flocking in

and perch on stems laced in crimson & lapis.

Listen to chittery voices swell in the hall

until, shells of walnut filled with tallow

hanging from vines of purple vinca

dim the hall in violet hues

and the curtain opens to the Mother's Mirabelle.

Layers of feathers of the wren and finch

adorn gentle wings of the Songbird's Faery.

In voice soft as dove she introduces her guest

as the Steward of the Mother and Protector of Nests.

When after the grateful twirping subsides,

Mirabelle harkens the first song of the nite.

A purdy tune sung by the Scarlet Cardinal Trio

accompanied by Bud the Bird on bass.

Sit back or hold tight whichever you are.

Ready yourself for Magnificence to begin

an enchanted spin.

High atop in the Concert Hall of the Cardinals!

What Size is Your Footprint?

Reduce, Reuse, Recycle, an Earth Day message from your Mother

Reader:

1. Is your footprint bigger than your shoe size?

2. Heavier than your weight?

3. Cover more ground than you can walk?

If You Answer Yes,

as many stewards do,

1. Measure matters of convenience.

2. Drop the calories of consumption.

3. Grow local ~ Buy local.

Tend the Mother's Soil

an Incantation

Blessed by God Thor

Reader, instruct the stewards to hold their list of New Green Habits and, recite:

God Thor,

in Thunderous times as these

when footprints exceed our size and weight

and global response too timid.

We call upon your strength and power

to pierce the skies with lightening strikes

that catch and hold attention

to a cause that's just and within our reach

and power to make a difference.

Reader, invite the stewards to go around the circle and read their lists of New Green Habits and then place them beside the vase of flowers.

All recite:

In honor of earth, I promise this day

to change the size of my footprint.

Word becomes deed when New Habits of Green

are practiced and firmly in place.

My commitment to Home will lead others to ponder

and change the size of their footprint.

Causing in time a much needed shift

from

matters of gobbling commerce

to sharing in sustaining measure

the treasures of the earth

shining bright in emerald green.

Tend the Soil Within

an Incantation

Blessed by Goddess Danu, an Irish Mother Goddess of Nature

Reader, instruct the stewards to hold their Tend the Soil List and, recite:

Goddess Danu,

Governess of the Growing Green

I bring my soil for sustenance.

For planted within~ a dream takes root.

Chosen by my heart's song,

my soul's longing

and the yearning of my body.

I feel the tingle of spreading wings

and listen to the call of my dream.

I see the faintest of contours beginning to show

and can taste the hint of tomorrow's nectar.

I've cultivated my dream as best I can

with nutrients of Hope, Passion, Knowledge and Perseverance.

I bring my soil to you, Goddess Danu

for your blessing and further sustenance.

Reader, invite the stewards to make their Tend the Soil requests to Goddess Danu and share them with the group if they like. Lay their list next to the doll.

Resume as Goddess Danu:

Steward of the Great Mother,

you honor me with your request.

The light of fruition burns bright within

basking your dream in prosperity.

All that you request is granted this day.

Tis my pleasure to Tend the Soil with you!

After the Earth Day celebration, open the circle with gratitude for our cultivated guests.

Goddess Danu

God Thor

the 4 Directions

Mirabelle, the Songbird's Faery

Scarlet Cardinal Trio

accompanied by,

Bud the Bird on bass

And, the Birds from Walhalla Ravine

<u>After the Ritual</u>

Place the Aventurine in the Health & Family Bagua of the home or room to lend support to your foundation. Post your lists~ Tend the Soil and New Green Habits somewhere visible to remind you of your commitment to dreams and the Mother.

All is Well Under Spring's Enchantment

~ Blessed Be ~

Chapter 9

K'UN BAGUA

#5

BELTANE

TAURUS

May

Discover the Divine Feminine

May's Sensual Nature

By May, spring's scintillating touch has all the senses abuzz. The dancing landscape is dominated by creeping phlox in every conceivable mood of pink. Princess pink dangles with the prim air of innocence while dance hall fuchsia's luxurious drape makes no such pretense. Ground cover, the Mother's jokester, humorously spreads over every outdoor surface imaginable. Rock walls, slopes, railroad ties and steps are the favorite drop offs for these creeping blooms. The sight of bushy azaleas bursting in vibrant reds is another illustration of spring's sensory buffet. Dazzling azaleas often trigger after dinner walks and drives through the neighborhood to show our family the flowering shrub we discovered earlier in the day. Our senses are stimulated almost to the point of overload and not just outdoors.

Opened windows welcome nature inside. We turn off the heat preferring the gentle nip in the air. Alarms are silenced as we rise to the lonesome coo of the morning dove. Nature's wakeup call gently coaxes the Mother's sleepy heads out from under the covers, but not before feeling the billowed breeze rustling through the cracked open window. The cool, slight puff of air that lands on the nose and spreads across the face, may be the Mother's most loving caress. The wind breezing in also brings the scent of the season which up until now, has been somewhat illusive. Spring's perfume is now strong enough to be inhaled in gulps, saturating our sense of taste and smell with the honey sweet nectar of lilac. Vases of this soft, plump blossom fill our rooms with the fragrant color of lavender. We adore lilac, so much so, that by the time they're spent, it seems more lilacs have graced our homes than can be counted on the trees outside.

The songbirds we welcomed home last month are busy building nests. Sometimes, they choose out of the ordinary places like gutters, corners of rooftops and protruding vents. Hanging plants also offer shelter and mimic the gentle swaying of trees. If you forget to take your winter wreath down don't be surprised if little house wrens borrow it for awhile. It's an honor for our homes to be chosen by our feathered friends and not unusual for descendants to take up residence in succeeding years. Watching eggs become hatchlings is a joyful spring pastime. Their swift maturation lends itself to keeping a daily check on their progress. There is something appealing about the scrawny, fuzzy nestlings when they first hatch. Their vulnerability brings out our maternal instincts. Once they fly away, it's often with a touch of sadness. Hopefully, they'll remain in the neighborhood and join in the morning serenades.

Around the middle part of the month, in what seems like a wink of an eye, the earth finally spins decisively away from winter, surprising us when it happens. Trees roll with the turn landing lush side out. As we observe this outer change through spring, we first notice the paleness of April's leaves. Later on in May, they seem darker but, not just because they changed colors. Yet, at a glance, that appears to be the case. Actually, as more and more leaves unfurl their sheer abundance deepens their veneer to a rich forest green. There is no better color in nature to symbolize 'all is well' with the planet. Flowering trees also signal spring's spin by budding in March, flowering in April and greening in May. When they complete their pirouette, we know summer will soon be here.

Once the season has taken hold, Mother nature begins conjuring up mating spells. Something in the air stirs us to mix love potions with natural aphrodisiacs creating enticing sensual brews. The season is known for its lusty appetites. Italian cuisine, hearty and comforting at winter's hearth, becomes the pasta of lovers served over bistro candlelight at a sidewalk cafe. The craving to linger over a romantic dinner increases as the cool night air whisks up our desires. Vanilla, a seemingly innocent bean, has a delicious, sensuous side. A dish of vanilla ice-cream sprinkled with crushed almonds and shared over dessert promises a taste of sweet, intimate love.

A Visit to the Wise Hazel Tree

The steward stands holding a fallen branch from the Wise Hazel Tree. The Tree watches mesmerized as the steward works his magic, cutting the branch to size, stripping the bark then, gently sanding out the rough edges and bumps. Smooth and strong he stands the branch up and begins attaching white and red ribbons to the top end. He pauses to count the number of ribbons and wonders if there are enough. "It's a fine looking Maypole," remarks a gnarly voice from behind. The steward turns toward the voice and looks into the virile face of God Cerne, consort of the Mother Goddess. "The Tree's been telling me about you these past months, so has the forest." The steward meets and holds Cerne's steady gaze as the God announces, "It has been decided." And, before the steward can ask for details, the God removes his antlered headdress, places it in the hands of the steward and disappears into the forest. The steward trembles in dawning recognition of the honor. The Wise Hazel Tree smiles at her son, pushing him toward the village balefire and says, "It's time." After walking a couple of steps, the steward turns back and asks the tree if she knows of a shop where he can pick up a little something for THE Maiden. She tells him, "Just inside the village of Knotville is a shop called, **Aincent Tradishuns.**" She chuckles and says, "You can't miss it." And, then cautions him, "Do remember the veil between the faery and human world is quite thin this time of year."

Branches of May's Wise Hazel Tree

Beltane~ May Day

Mother's Day

K'un~ Love & Relationship Bagua

Vibration of 5

Sun in Taurus

Throughout the magnificent month of May, the Mother breathes life into nature's creations. Each breath presents the opportunity to awaken the divine feminine within. The discovery of the divine feminine is not complete without the courtship and consummation of the feminine with the masculine. Through this dance, men and women remain equal. The surefooted ones are those who spiritually and consciously exercise both their inner feminine and masculine natures. Divine manifestation requires both. Every spring we are invited to discover the coexistence of our dual nature. After which, life unfolds differently. For the initiate, the discovery of our dual nature may go something like this~

The courtship of the inner feminine and masculine begins with the willing intake of the Mother's breath. Prior to this, our divine yin and yang were acquainted as familiar strangers. Once the breath takes hold they become more aware of one another, but may continue to function independently and at times in opposition.

Until, one day, they awaken then close their eyes and drift back together to the in-between where the Mother calls through the stillness. Yin and yang begin to listen. In soft voice, whispers really, the Mother encourages yin to open as wide as can be to the gift of the moment. Yang, listening too, chooses to linger, resisting the impulse to act.

The voice suggests they move forward together. A discussion ensues and an agreement is made to watch for signs of the day and act accordingly. After more days have passed, yin and yang feel more comfortable creating life together and begin each day with goals in hand and means in the making. United at last, life settles into a balanced ebb and flow.

Before long, life senses a larger undercurrent. Trusting and curious, life relaxes into the tide that springs from universal waters. Life flows into the vast, immense and limitless world of divine possibilities where we complete our individuation within a global womb. When ready, the gushing waters of our rebirth spill onto fields of dreams, nurturing life within and around the world. We open our eyes and inhale the Mother's breath. This time it's effortless.

We rejoice in the discovery of the divine feminine and Unity of the Goddess and God during the lighthearted holiday of Beltane also known as May Day. Traditionally, the Goddess in maiden phase loses both her virginity and becomes a mother in wait during the ritual at Beltane Eve. According to ancient lore, the union between the Goddess and God Cerne is enacted by a young maiden and her consort. McCoy describes May Day activities, such as weaving ribbons around the maypole, as one of the symbols of their fertile consummation. It also signifies her transition from one phase of the Goddess to another, the maiden to the mother. Our ritual invites both maidens and consorts to discover their own divine yin as we dance together around the maypole.

In addition to the maypole, the balefire is another symbol of this pagan holy day and serves a similar purpose. The balefire ignites the revelry. Dancers with bells at their feet twirl to music around the fire raising the sexual energy to a fevered pitch. The fertile current creates the perfect moment to make a promise to the self or another by leaping over the flames. The promise can also be made by jumping over a broomstick. Fire as a purifier also creates the opportunity to cleanse by drawing ritual smoke over the body. In older times, when crops fell more easily to disease and mercurial weather, ashes from this holy fire were scattered over the fields to ensure a bountiful growing season.

May Day is steeped in mystical lore, superstition and maternal devotion. Flowers as symbols are also important at Beltane. Maidens are adorned with wreaths of flowers signifying the divine union. Children also wear wreaths to ward off the mischievous faery folk. May baskets are filled with flowers according to the desired spiritual power. This means, that May baskets can represent more than the mating of the Goddess and God. Within a larger pagan context, filling the basket can signify the maiden's maturity to wholeness and command of her personal power. This month's ritual helps each of us discover and nurture our own divine feminine to sustain life~ ours, the Great Mother and all her children. We're not alone in our desire to honor the Mother and protect her children. In the states, Mother's Day, is a holiday in which we shower our maternal beloveds with gratitude and well wishes

Numerology's connection to symbols plays an unusually significant role this month. When the number five energy is pulled through May's spiritual purpose, it helps enliven the feminine voice and perspective individually and collectively. The pentagram is an interesting connection to the month's vibration. This pagan five pointed star is most often used as a unifying symbol of the four directions and spirit. The star is made more powerful when it is placed within a circle as a pentacle. The pentacle reminds us to honor May's place in the Great Mother's global circle of life.

Feng Shui, another ancient tradition, is particularly suited for a month emphasizing the union of yin and yang energies. The Love & Relationship Bagua, the receptive K'un, has a twofold purpose of nurturing our relationship with the self. First, loving the self is an important aspiration in its own right. It is key to our lives unfolding as we have envisioned. Secondly, who we attract as a mate will reflect our ability to love the self. The person will be there for us to the degree to which we are there for ourselves. When we are able to fill ourselves with love and purpose, we are in a position of power and more able to attract a mate of equal standing. That's not to say that we have to be in a significant relationship. We may choose a solitary path or a mated one, each are fulfilling. In either case, we must learn to fully care for the self. Regardless of sexual orientation, or whether we're mated or not, the Great Mother needs her stewards to be strong and self loving. We have a lot to change in the world.

Saving the sweetest tradition for last, we come to Taurus, our Sun kissed sign of the month. Blessed by Goddess Venus, our Beltane celebration is aesthetically pleasing, artfully done and properly seasoned with natural aphrodisiacs. Venus, our Goddess of love, instills a bit of dreamy romance into an otherwise practical and stubborn sign. Under her influence, the energy becomes pampering and supportive. As an Earth sign, nurturing Taurus lends a hand in creating a healthy environment. This brings us to another aspect of the spiritual purpose this month, the necessity of Divine Unity to achieve wholeness within and without. Advocacy for the planet requires a strong sense of self, duty and persevering action.

Lapis-Lazuli, a companion stone of our Sun kissed sign, can help us achieve all aspects of our spiritual intention. Its midnight blue color resonates deep within the soul. It is a great tool for spiritual pathwork. Lapis opens intuition and leads us to the seat of our personal power. Once we tap into inner knowledge, our self awareness is more easily expressed through the spoken word and deed. One of the reasons the stone was selected is the emphasis on eliminating suffering without martyrdom, the ultimate compromise of the self. In our efforts to make the world a better place, we certainly don't want to get lost in the cause.

Prepare for May's Ritual

If possible, perform ritual either on April 30th~Beltane Eve, May

1st, or on Mother's Day. The ritual lends itself quite nicely outside

with a gathering of men, women and children alike.

~ Seasonings for the Wise Hazel Tree's May Brew ~

For the Ritual Altar~

An Altar Cloth

A Midnight Blue Candle for Goddess Bloddueth and God Cerne

A Smudge Stick of Sage

A Bowl to Withstand the Fire's Flames

Lapis-Lazuli for May's Intent

To Stand Next to a Symbol of Spirit

A Bloddueth Doll

A Broomstick

A Basket of Fresh Flowers

Maypole (for the altar or outside)

Your Mother's Day Promise

Vanilla Crème Pie and Spring Blend Tea

Your Wand Made from a Stick

Tasks Before the Ritual

1. Smell the flowers.

2. Fill the house with blooms from the yard.

3. Pick a tree in your yard or neighborhood and watch it roll with spring's turn and land lush side out.

4. Court, so to speak, your inner yin throughout the month with simple gestures of love.

5. Think of two loving promises you're willing to make this year~ One for the maternal beloveds in your life whomever they are. And, another promise for Mother Earth.

6. Make or embellish the doll to honor Goddess Bloddueth.

7. Make a maypole, either, as an altar decoration or to dance around. The traditional ribbon colors are red (for the God) and white (for the Goddess).

8. Select a charm that represents your Divine Unity and attach it to the wand.

The Day of the Ritual

Prepare the Ritual Feast

Vanilla makes this crème pie a natural aphrodisiac for Beltane celebrations. Brew a cup of spring blend tea with your charged water and serve it hot or over ice.

Placement of the Altar ~

Lay the altar cloth on the table

For the Four Directions~

Wand in the East

Sage and Burning Bowl in the South

Tea and Pie in the West

Basket of Flowers in the North

In the center of the altar, place the midnight blue candle

for Goddess Bloddueth and God Cerne

Arrange the symbol of spirit and the Lapis-Lazuli near the blue candle

Set the Bloddueth doll before the blue candle with the maypole beside her (if inside)

Lay your Mother's Day promises next to the doll

Lay the broomstick in the East

Scatter the altar with all things divinely feminine

Time to Center and Smudge ~

Cast the Circle ~

Invite the Directions ~

Reader:

Welcome Direction of East, Spirit of Spring's Scent. Lilacs fill the air
with the color of lavender. Slowly breathe in soft, purple, fragrant wisps.
Breathe in again~ feel the spiral descent of caressing scent.

Welcome Direction of South, Spirit of Promises. Cooing in the ear, a kiss on the lips,
murmurs of love~ the light touch of passion and the sensual promise of more to come.

Welcome Direction of West, Spirit of New Life. Care for tender shoots of planted dreams.
Watch as they unfurl their veneer to lush green. Rejoice in the unfolding of desires claimed.
(Have a bit of tea and pie.)

Welcome Direction of North, Spirit of the Divine Feminine. Receptive
K'un~ dwell in the moment, will yourself to love, listen to the stories
of others. Discover the Mother~ the wise nurturer.

Welcome Goddess Bloddueth and God Cerne, Spirit of Divine Unity. Green
Woman and Green Man of the Forest we are honored by your presence.
Bless our celebration of May. Lighten our heart and quicken our step as
we weave within and without the Divine Union of Yin and Yang.
Light the midnight blue candle.

The Shop of Aincent Tradishuns
Proprietress, Talya, the Gypsy Faery

Reader:

Just inside the Village of Knotville stands a Maple tree five stories tall. The Wise Hazel
Tree claims she first made His acquaintance when they were saplings together. Visitors to the
village can see the Maple from miles away making it a particularly handsome sight in the fall.
Now, unbeknownst to regular humans and only known to those with the gift of sight, there is
a shop located just inside the oval shaped knot at the base of the tree.

The story goes that as soon as the knot appeared long, long ago, the O'Bucklae family
settled in and never left. This was pretty unusual considering they're connected to a gypsy
clan of faeries. Apparently, the matriarch, Maudevine, caught herself a fine looking man, a
knight from Camelot at Beltane Eve and promised to give up her roaming ways if he promised
not to cross back into the other world. Except for the one cross forest trip every midsummer,
Sir Thomas lived true to his promise. After their hand fasting, they set up shop inside the knot
and built living quarters above.

*Even as a child, Maudevine was into all manner of paranormal goings-on. The kind of shop they opened up the following May Day was no surprise to her family. Maudevine, with the help of the fine finishing skills of her man, Sir Thomas turned that knot into the **Shop of Aincent Tradishuns.** It turned out to be one of the best things that ever happened to the village folk. Central Knotville was a pagan stronghold from way back. Faery folk and humans alike enjoyed nothing better than a good ole, earthy frolic under a moonlit sky.*

*Until the shop opened, many villagers made a trip out of county to pick up accoutrements needed for the various Sabbats. You can imagine the delight in discovering a shop close to home with everything needed for every season, every month and every holiday. And what a spiritual adventure it was for Maudevine to turn her shop around every first day of the month. People lined up outside the knot at 5:55 in the morning to catch the **First Day Sales.** For many years, Maudevine and her man lived a fine life indeed.*

A fine life, that is, until they got overly old and could no longer run the shop. Maudevine was determined to keep the shop open. She believed it was her family's destiny to provide Central Knotville with accessible divinity supplies. And so, she and Sir Thomas decided to transfer proprietorship to a granddaughter with similar interests in all things divine. This set the stage for succeeding transfers to be made to the granddaughter most like Maudevine. Given the faery matriarch's fertile lineage, it won't surprise you to know that there's never been a shortage of candidates. Which brings us to the current shop owner, Talya~ the Gypsy Faery and the telling of tonight's Beltane Eve story.

Now this shop owner's 'somethin to behold'! Talya's quick silver tongue can build you up, or cut you down to size, leaving you laughing either way. Cute as a faerybug, Talya is shorter than most, with brown, almond shaped eyes and two round tufts of chestnut hair that sit up high on her head making her look at least five wings of an inch taller. She mostly never met a stranger she didn't like, a quality she got from her Great, Great Grandmother, Maudevine. Village folk say she has the patience of a Goddess. But, if you cross her she grows into the imposing stature of one, not unlike her favorite aunt. She has a bohemian style about her and is fond of wearing ethnic jewelry and pins advertising one cause or another. Come fall, she usually sticks a couple of leaves in her hair referring to it as her Maple Coif. Today, in honor of Beltane she's wearing lilac died hemp wear, twinkling stars on midnight blue wings, a tiny yin yang nose stud, and a little wreath of burgundy verbena and white mums nestled crookedly around her chestnut tufts.

Now, onto tonight's story! Early evening around 5:00, the village of Knotville was a twitter with excitement. The first of the balefires was causing quite a stir. Folks were bustling here and there putting the finishing touches on the May Eve celebration. When the steward crossed over into Knotville, he felt a decidedly yummy sensation deep in his belly. He noticed the townsfolk running up and down the hill with odd looking knapsacks laden with ribbons, bells, baskets and food. The food was exotic dishes seasoned with basil, rosemary and thyme. It was the best smelling food ever and caused his belly to flip over sideways. A couple of the young maidens glanced his way drawing his attention away from his nose. He wondered if perhaps one of them was THE maiden.

*The color periwinkle caught his attention out of the corner of his eye. He walked over to the tall Maple and traced his finger along the wide periwinkle lip of the knot. As soon as he ended where he began, the steward was standing inside the **Shop of Aincent Tradishuns.** The Gypsy Faery said, "It's not really that color. For some reason, folks with the sight see it that way. Hi, I'm Talya. You must be the steward the Wise Hazel Tree told me about. The antlers kinda give you away. You can set the headdress and maypole down next to the counter." Seeing his woozy look, like not all of him made it through the knot, Talya softened her voice and said, "It takes a moment for humans to adjust to coming through."*

Once he got his bearings, he began looking around the shop. Next to the register hanging off a coat rack were hundreds of Cocoon Knapsacks. Talya said, "They're reusable and fit nicely over wings and such. They hold a lot more than you think. I get them from the Larva Society of Central Knotville. They donate them once or twice a year." "How do you get them back," the steward asked? "I've got a turnaround spell on them. When you're done, just say thank you and poof they're back on the rack." Talya answered, pleased with her ingenuity!

"You've got a big nite ahead. How can I help?" Talya asked. The steward said, "I want to give THE maiden a gift in thanks for agreeing to the Joining Ceremony. But, I have no clue what to get. I don't even know who she is." Talya told him that God Cerne was in earlier getting something for Goddess Bloddueth and fessed up about THE Maiden. Talya swore telling the secret had nothing to do with the aniseed candy on the counter. "It doesn't much

matter now if I tell you, you'll know soon enough. Her name is Luna Giggling Buddha." He smiled at the sound of her name. "Yeah, it's a great name. She's part witch and part Buddhist. She's lovely too...with long, wavy hair the color of moonlight and powder blue eyes." Talya informed him wistfully.

*"But, her soft looks are deceiving. She's no puff muffin. She's the editor of the **Feminique Quarterly.** It's a really cool magazine with lots of seasonal stuff~ fun fests, Sabbat and Buddhist events and usually a socio-political editorial. Luna's really into the global political scene. In fact, the quarterly just went international. It was picked up by the **Consolidated Faery Network** last week," Talya continued a little more seriously. The steward's interest and respect was piqued as Talya told him other little bits about his Joining mate.*

"Well, the Sun's going down, you better get looking," Talya told the steward. He glanced around the shop and noticed that except for the barrel next to the register selling Ostara Whatnots, everything else seemed to have something to do with May Day. As the room got lighter, he looked up and saw the Pentacle Chandelier hanging from braided ribbon. A vanilla scented candle sat on each edge of the five pointed star. One by one the candles were lit by Talya's wand from across the room. She also lit the beeswax tapers in the window boxes filled with creeping phlox on either side of the knot and behind the counter. Talya handed him a cup of coffee to sip while he browsed. He noticed the flavored brew of the month was Amaretto Cream.

*The steward decided to go left and work his way around the shop. Wavy shelves painted periwinkle were carved into the circular walls. Barrels in midnight blue stood in front of a particular sector. The first one contained pine maypoles. The shelf behind it held yards of white and red ribbon cut in perfect 105" lengths. The sign said they were **Guaranteed to Unify.** He was over half way around in the **K'un Sector** when he noticed some cut jasmine and heather had fallen out of a basket from the top crest of the shelf. As he stooped to pick them up, he bumped his knee on the bottom shelf upending another basket filled with Maple wood chips. "You alright over there?" Talya called out. "Yep, just being klutzy. What are the woodchips for," he asked? "The blank ones?" "Yeah," he replied. "If you firebrand your intended's name on a woodchip from this Maple tree and throw it into a balefire your lover is* *yours for life,"* Talya answered. *"Does it work,"* the steward wondered out loud? *"I wouldn't be here if it didn't,"* she laughed.

Which started Talya on the story of Maudevine and Sir Thomas. Before the whole story was told, the sound of tinkling blue bells dangling off the left side of the fetching indigo feather hat of the next customer got them back on task. *"You're in the **Love Potions** Sector,"* Talya told him. *"Go check out the black licorice in **Natural Aphrodisiacs** while I help Duchess St. DatilWise."* The steward circled around some more until, he finally found rolls and rolls of uncut licorice. According to the sign, the licorice was sold in lengths of **15 Minute Interludes** with the price break at~ **All Night Long**. He had no idea how much to buy and settled on the **All Night Long** special figuring he could bring back any unused licorice tomorrow.

The steward had one more sector left and hoped he could find a couple of more things for Luna. As he rounded on the knot, he noticed a glass case holding **Lapis-Lazuli Appurtenance.** There were tinctures for the throat, perfume bottles with lapis stoppers, tiny gazing spheres, lapis point wands and all kinds of polished lapis jewelry. He spotted a delicate anklet with lapis beads, silver crescent Moons and chubby, little Buddha's strung on the finest spider webbing. He was sure he had found the perfect present for Luna.

One more gift and he was done. Earlier, he had seen a young sapling in the center of the shop decorated with sparkling twig pentacles, holding maiden wreaths. He called out to Talya and asked, *"What flower would be best?"* Duchess St. DatilWise answered instead, *"I've always thought purple violets were quite nice for this occasion."* She held his gaze steadily and then said, *"They promote fidelity. That one with the midnight blue ribbon would look quite lovely against Luna's blonde hair."*

He took his presents up to the counter and waited until the Duchess had completed her purchase. He overheard them double-checking the Call Ahead Party Favor order. The Duchess has lots of petites and had special ordered 11 glazed raspberry cups with dusted faery candy. Talya was telling the Duchess that the really fun part was creating handles for the cups in the initials of her petites. *"Let's count them to make sure I made enough. Let's see, you wanted 2 J's, 3 E's, 2 G's, 2 K's and 2 P's.**"** "That's right,"* the Duchess replied. *"Look at them, how sweet! I know I won't be able to wait till tomorrow to hand them out. Steward, why* *don't you go ahead of me. I just remembered I've been out of datil pepper since last Ostara. I'll need some for tonight. Goddess Bloddueth wants me to spice up the Beltane feast."*

When he was done settling up, the steward thanked Talya for all her help and told her he hoped he would see her tonight. Talya said, "You'll see me alright. I've got my eye on someone and winked as she rubbed the woodchip in her pocket." On his way out, he picked up the spring issue of the **Feminique Quarterly**. *He placed it along with some balefire kindling and his gifts inside a cocoon knapsack, grabbed his antlers, maypole and left through the knot. His eyes adjusted to the dark just as a long stretch of village folk began making their way up to the hill, where 5 blazing balefires lit up the dark sky. The May King took a deep breath and walked up the hillside ready to join his May Queen.*

A Joining Ceremony

of

Steward, the May King and Luna, the May Queen

Officiating~ Goddess Bloddueth and God Cerne

Reader, recite as Goddess Bloddueth:

> *Sons, Daughters & Children of Knotville,*
>
> *come forth and encircle the Sun & Moon.*
>
> *sons, spread out creating the outer ring.*
>
> *daughters, do the same to form the inner ring.*
>
> *children, the Mother's sacred~ circle the innermost ring.*
>
> *3 Rings,*
>
> *Father, Mother, Child,*
>
> *separate energies,*
>
> *maturing alone,*
>
> *supported in the standing company of your reflection.*
>
> *Women, join hands.*
>
> *Luna, come forth and stand before me.*
>
> *Daughter, of the Moon,*

reflection of the Mother,

What do you bring to this union?

Reader as Luna:

Goddess Bloddueth, Divine Feminine

I am a Woman

strong & capable.

A voice for the unheard,

a student of the mysteries,

a loving touch.

Reader, recite as God Cerne:

Men, Join Hands.

Steward, come forth and stand before me.

Son of the Sun,

reflection of the father

What do you bring to this union?

Reader, recite as the Steward:

God Cerne, Divine Masculine

I am a Man

strong & loving.

A protector of the unarmed,

a steward of the forest,

a visible touch.

Reader, resume as Goddess Bloddueth and God Cerne:

Men, Join the Circle of Women.

Steward, place the Maiden Wreath upon her head and the jewelry around her ankle.

Luna, place the antlered headdress upon the head of your joining mate.

Join Hands and State your Promise to each other~

Reader, resume as Luna and the Steward:

> *We join in reverence to Divine Unity*
>
> *our internal union of yin & yang,*
>
> *now reflected in the other.*
>
> *We promise this eve*
>
> *to nurture the global circle of new life.*

Reader, resume as Goddess Bloddueth and God Cerne:

> *You may now jump over the broomstick to seal your promise.*

All Together:

> *So Mote it Be ~*

Reader, resume as Goddess Bloddueth and God Cerne:

> *Children, Join the Circle of Divine Unity*
>
> *and enjoy Luna and her Steward's*
>
> *first dance around the maypole.*

Reader, after the dance, invite the stewards to share their promises to their maternal beloveds and Mother Earth. Seal the promise made by jumping over the broomstick.

Sparkling Spiral Sayer

a Seer Gains Her Sight

Reader:

The last dance did her in. Tired and spent, the mother left the circle sleepy and full. After making sure the Duchess was watching the children, the mother wandered to the edge of the forest for a little cat nap. The distant scent of honeysuckle drew her to a little mound not more than a foot tall underneath a blooming Hawthorne. She laid down under the tree and soon fell deep asleep.

It was too dark for the mother to notice, but this particular mound was home to a family of faeries. They were a benevolent clan of seers who practiced all manner of divination. As soon as the mother fell into a soft slumber, the Goddess Appointed Seer Initiate, Sean Domhan softly kissed the sleeping eyes of the mother. At once their transport appeared. Catching the spiral with one hand and the mother's with the other, they gently swirled deep into the earth, to the otherworld.

Sean let go of the mother's hand upon landing. She awoke standing at the honeysuckle entrance of a labyrinth encircled by an Oak grove. The doorway into the mysteries was clear, the beginning of the walk visible to the mother. Sensing her questions, Sean answered with, "The Great Mother must have chosen you. Once a year at Beltane Eve, she picks a mother whose inner sight is capable of carrying Her vision across the lands over the next year.

There is no need for worries or fear. You wouldn't be here if you weren't ready. Stand in the threshold and breathe deep. With each breath envision your inner light growing until bright enough to light your labyrinth journey. When the way is illuminated, you may pass through. I will wait here to spiral you home when you're finished." The mother squeezed his hand and took a deep breath. In time, she opened her eyes and stepped forward onto the lit path.

~ The Journey ~

As familiar as she was with a labyrinth, somehow, this first step felt different. The thought occurred to her that tonight's journey would take her to an even deeper level within the self. With the next step, she whispered, "I am open to what lies beneath." This became her mantra.

As the mother walked on, she felt less entrapped by the abyss of regret. The sensation of fullness spread through her limbs. With the next step, she whispered, "My life begins anew with each light of dawn." This became her mantra.

Bits of light escaped from her heart. Sparkles of joy welled up and leapt twinkling into the night. With the next step, she whispered, "The Mother's work kindles the smiles of her children." This became her mantra.

In silence, she walked. Stirrings made of hot, malleable iron sizzled in her belly. With the next step, she spoke out loud, "I forge my life in accordance with the Mother." She repeated this mantra, until arriving at the center.

Golden light streaked in silver welcomed the mother. Seer faeries with illumined pentacle wings danced along oaken branches closest to the labyrinth. The mother turned once around absorbing the well wishes of the otherworld. Facing the light, she bowed her head to receive the Wreath of Heather~ a symbol of Feminine Power. In reverence, the Great Mother pronounced, "You have done well my child. I am most pleased."

"Dear Woman, do you know the vision you are to protect and carry this year?" "I believe so," the Sparkling Spiral Saver answered confidently. "This night~ I discovered what lies *beneath was ever present, a constant source of the Mother's love~ Regret lives in darkness. It has no power in the light of dawn~ Joyful service nourishes the hearts of children and makes the stars come out~ And last, I am an open vessel of my own making which I willingly fill with your light. I am ready." "So you are," intoned the Great Mother.*

The Great Mother placed a black and purple Goddess shawl around the mother's shoulders. And, Bestowed this Divine Blessing~

May your inner feminine shine bright across the lands,

Spreading the Mother's Love.

May you always greet the light of dawn,

Receiving the Mother's Grace.

May your heart sprinkle the children with bits of joy,

Creating rising Stars of Tomorrow.

May your life inspire others to journey within,

Discovering Their Own Divine Feminine.

Go forth from this night as Sparkling Spiral Sayer, the Mother's Seer.

The Great Mother watched the newly appointed seer walk the labyrinth back to the entrance, infusing her with enough divine love to sustain her till next they meet.

At the end of the walk, the Mother's Seer sensed the presence of Sean Domhan before she saw him resting against the threshold. She offered him her hand and together they ascended the spiral back to the land of the human. This time with her sparkling eyes wide open.

Enjoy the feast~ dance, drink and be merry. When you can spin no

more, open the circle with gratitude for our enchanting guests~

Goddess Bloddueth

God Cerne

the 4 Directions

Maudevine & Sir Thomas

Talya, the Gypsy Faery

Duchess St. DatilWise

Luna Giggling Buddha & the Steward

Sparkling Spiral Sayer

& Sean Domhan, the Goddess Appointed Seer Initiate

<u>After the Ritual</u>

Find a place of honor within the Love & Relationship Bagua of the home or room
to keep your promises and Lapis-Lazuli. Slip the stone into your pocket when
you're in need of the Mother's touch. All is Well Under Spring's Enchantment

~ Blessed Be ~

All Is Well in the Shade of the Tree

Summer~ A Time To:

Nurture New Life ~ June

Foster Growth ~ July

Prepare to Harvest ~ August

A Summer Essay

Children grow into adolescents who in turn leave the nest as young adults. In human time, many years pass before we see the fruits of our parental labor. Within the natural world, the growing season encompasses a similar passage yet yields a harvest in a much shorter span of time. Both images are helpful in understanding the purpose of summer. Seeds of dreams planted during spring, sprout as toddlers in June requiring constant watch and nurturing. As our dreams become independent teens in July, we strike a balance between a watchful eye and encouraging a certain amount of freedom. This allows our dreams to materialize in their own way. When the first of the three harvest Sabbats arrives in August, we are ready to begin unveiling our dreams. As any parent of a young adult knows, the run to adulthood is in stages with frequent trips to home base. So, we too will continue to fine tune our dreams over the next few months until the final harvest in the fall.

Although the growing season is important, we mix our tending responsibilities with the sheer fun and exuberance of the season. There is no mistaking the other purpose of summer, to relax and enjoy the company of family and friends. It is a season of adventurous camaraderie and patio cook outs with grilled garden vegetables and ice cold watermelon. Work doesn't necessarily slow down, yet, we allow ourselves time off for long weekends and vacations. Our traditions reappear with the Sun. Reunions, annual trips with friends, return visits to treasured spots are marked on the calendar. Our excitement is barely contained as the dates draw near. If we have children in our lives, our world revolves around camp and summer fun rather than school events. Daylight stretches beyond bedtime, thus lengthening the amount of time we have for ourselves and each other.

Under sunny skies, the earth trips over itself with countless species of vegetation, critters and bugs. Helped along by the rattling and rolling thunder of summer storms, every inch of yard is painted in primary water colors. Pots of pansies are replaced with purple petunias and red geraniums. Perennials crowd each other for more space to show themselves off, with some spreading out and others reaching up. If they leave any gaps at all we fill the space with annuals, yard art and bird baths. We create backyard retreats to reflect the natural world. We don't necessarily want to share our homes with toads, squirrels and deer, but we seem to love metallic or ceramic renditions whimsically placed where they can do no harm.

Summer has the remarkable ability to rev us up and chill us out. Both of these natural energy cycles are caused by the Sun. As nature lets loose in outrageous splendor, we too cut loose in carefree abandon. Eventually, though, we begin to wilt under the constant scrutiny of the Sun. Too much heat causes us to seek shade and shelter to cool off, rest a spell and gaze a bit. Then, we're off again on another escapade. What a wonderful time of the year it is, the lazy, zany days of summer. All is Well in the Shade of the Tree.

Chapter 10

June

Nurture New Life

Carolann Gregoire, MSW

June's Sensual Nature

We slide into summer as early June brings on the heat. Our bodies remember humidity when cool spring evenings turn into muggy summer mornings. Those of us vulnerable to muggy mercury turn air conditioners on once the temperature rises above eighty-five. After turning the switch, it's difficult to think of June as spring any longer. Most would agree that summer begins with the last day of school. Afterwards, observers of the Sun's ascent to its zenith crest at Litha, the Summer Solstice, can enjoy the Sun's rise to dominance. Once the wheel has turned, we alternately bless and curse the Sun depending upon if we're basking in radiant sunshine, or burning from its blistering rays. We manage alright as long as we have someplace to cool off, in the shade, in front of a fan, or sitting on the porch.

Landscaped lawns and dressed up porches offer endless amusement during early morning and late evening walks in the neighborhood. The personality of the homeowner comes through in the pristine care or neglect of the property. The average person falls somewhere in between. Choosing the right plants for a garden is tricky. There is much to consider: soil, sunlight, color, height, maintenance and compatibility with others. It's a lot of work, but the loveliness of a summer lawn is worth the effort. Although, equally appealing is the madcap scattering of wildflowers occupying an entire front yard. Another charming feature of the summertime whimsy are eclectically outfitted porches. These outside living spaces offer the chance to mix and match indoor and outdoor décor with an air of old world grace. We drape throws over swings and scarves over tables to match the roof and potted plants.

Summer may be the time of year in which we live in season the most easily. We soak up the outdoors. Kids and adults find all manner of ways to stay outside. We sign up for leagues, catch the occasional pickup game and sit on the deck with a cool one. The play of children is at its best in the hot months. When coaxed outdoors away from indoor temptations they explore their neighborhood on bikes, make up street games and look for treasures hidden in creek beds. Our intrinsic connection with the natural world corresponds with the hours of available Sun time. Our imagination inspired by the Great Mother's mystery and beauty offers endless moments of joy.

The trees of June help us adjust our mood to the luxuriant rhythm of the season. The bushy branches sway to and fro without a care in the world; like us, they respond appreciatively to a windy day. The quicksilver turn of the wheel leaves nature a bit overheated. Many of the Mother's creatures seek refuge under Her sheltering branches. Some of the best memories of childhood recall rainy moments under leafy canopies and listening to the crescendo of woodwinds during a storm. The Great Mother chose well when selecting trees as the Wise Guardians of the natural world.

A Visit to the Wise Hazel Tree

Coll, the faun stood beside the Wise Hazel Tree kicking up dirt with his hoof. "Be careful. The steward just planted the garden," the Tree gently admonished. "I am," snapped Coll. "It's just that Hazel's trying to fasten a wreath of cat-o'-nine-tails to my horn and its tickling my ear." "Hazel, quit pestering your friend dear," the Tree corrected. "Give me one more second okay, got it" giggled the Tree's littlest guardian faery as she flew from the faun to a branch and onto one of the Tree's twisty roots. Teetering a bit on the landing, the faery steadied herself with her tawny brown butterfly wings with gray spots. Her fuzzy dandelion hair went flying as she skipped down the root teasing, "Collie's got a new tollie," and then disappeared underground, the dirt muffling her final taunt. The Tree couldn't help laughing as Coll turned around to see his nub of a tail was now long and bushy, swishing the flies off the grilled leftovers from the picnic. The steward hid his smile from Coll as he quickly gathered up the veggie burgers, summer squash and corn salsa. The Tree stopped herself before reminding the steward to take care with the last jar of salsa from the Mother's cupboard.

Branches of June's Wise Hazel Tree

Litha~ Summer Solstice

Father's Day

Tui~ Children & Creativity Bagua

Vibration of 6

Sun in Gemini

Litha is the longest day in the Great Mother's Wheel of Life. We spend the dark months reaching for the Sun as it makes its slow ascent to the Summer Solstice. For one day we enjoy its peak at Midsummer celebrations. Then, the Sun begins what seems like a quicker descent to the Winter Solstice. It feels counterintuitive to celebrate the hot Sun early in the season knowing it also marks the beginning of the waning time of the year. Yet, it does signal this pivotal change. We see the return of the Oak and Holly Kings as they rival for supremacy once again. Winning, the Holly King throws the Oak King out of the castle transforming the estate into its counterpart, Midsummer Manor. We relish the Sun for as long as we have Him. And as our ancestors did before us, honor the Father in the sky.

In our celebrations, we also pray for a blessed growing season. Early summer is the time of the year when so much happens simultaneously in nature. The earth is fertile above and below the surface. A few seeds are still fermenting below, some plants may be just breaking ground, while others are ready for picking. Because of this early bounty, another name for Litha is Gathering Day. Summer squash and certain aromatic plants with magical properties are ready for harvest. Edain McCoy informs us that June is a good time of the year to restock our shelves with love and fertility potions. Healers of different traditions gather herbs, hanging them to dry for future medicinal use.

Furthermore, seeking protection is an important aspect of this Sabbat. We want to protect our dreams and fertile wombs to ensure a bountiful harvest. Faeries, who ordinarily help the Mother care for the natural world can also be mischievous. Old customs sought protection from their impish antics, especially, at Litha when it was believed that faery power reflected the Sun's ruling position in the sky. Talismans were often crafted resembling the Sun for many purposes including safe travels, healthy livestock and crops even, amulets for pets and familiars.

It's a busy time for humans as well. Weddings, pregnancy, caring for children and our growing dreams fill up our June calendar. The ritual of Litha acknowledges these passages and responsibilities. According to McCoy, June may be the favored wedding month because of our pagan heritage. In days past, May weddings were ill-advised because of the sacred union of the God and Goddess at Beltane. Wedding traditions today are reminiscent of pagan fertility customs such as sharing the wedding cake, tossing rice and carrying the bride over the threshold. The Sun's dominance in the sky and role in the growing season also ensures the Father's rightful place in the creation of life. Litha fulfills a responsibility to men by helping them prepare for fatherhood.

Like the Sun's nurturing of the natural world, parents promote the fullest expression of their child's human existence. We guide the child's unique light allowing for the soul's brightest manifestation in this world. The responsibility to protect and encourage is a balance not easily achieved by parents. The innocent exuberance and inquisitive nature of children is sometimes squelched in our efforts to shield them from the dark. The evolving relationship between parent and child is a lifelong journey of holding and letting go. To survive in these times our children must learn to stand on their own, help others and, do so with love and integrity intact. As we discover how to be green gardeners of crops and dreams, we must also pursue what it means to be green guardians of our children. These discoveries are the spiritual quest of Litha.

Feng Shui can help. The Children & Creativity Bagua~ Tui reminds us to approach our duties with a light touch. Too often, adult responsibilities are literally tackled. In our hustling through life, we forget what it means to simply be and enjoy each day. We may find our children's noisy existence annoying rather than inspiring~ their energy exhausting, not invigorating. Why? Because we have forgotten to nurture our own internal wonder and innocence. This loss is most unfortunate as the best in us is childlike. The acceptance of good, joy of the moment and trust in the possible is sometimes lost in maturity. Children unencumbered by the weight of material chains and the illusion of separation naturally experience our connection to spirit. The spiritual energy of this Bagua can help us return to our own innocence of being and sense of divine purpose. Once there, we're in a better place to nurture and encourage the new growth of our dreams. As guardians of children, we are more able to support the unfolding of their divine natures.

Numerology, another ancient tradition, also helps us accept our responsibilities. There is a lot riding on our ability to care for dreams, the Mother's children and her crops. The number six resonates with the energy we need this month. It is an intensely laden number. Matters of the home are of the utmost importance as is service to humankind. Keeping an eye to balance, this synchronous energy supplies us with all that is necessary to protect and ably respond to whatever arises.

Astrology can lend us a hand with the busy month of June. Gemini, our Sun kissed sign of the month knows a bit about multi-tasking. The sign has been blessed or cursed, depending on your perspective, with the desire to engage in as many things as possible, all at once. Curious and bright, the air sign's energy propels us to seek the new. Once the experience has been lived from all sides, Gemini moves on. This can leave the impression of fickleness and superficiality. Another interpretation is that Gemini emotions do run deep but the energy prefers to flow with the current of a new stream. Orange Calcite, the selected companion stone assists in stabilizing the scattered mind of the sign. The stone distinguishes the important from the unimportant which helps Gemini retain the heart of the experience. Gemini is the social butterfly who enjoys a myriad of friends made from her various adventures. This aspect of the sign fits nicely with the lighthearted camaraderie of summer.

Mercury is the ruling planet of Gemini which underscores the sign's able communication skills and interest in travel. Mercury's energy has been described as quicksilver. This helps explain Gemini's multi-tasking talent. It also explains the downside of this willful energy. If we're not careful when under Mercury's influence we can experience instances of miscommunication and travel mishaps. It's best to handle this planet's energy with kid gloves, or better yet, considering all the important work that must get done this month, let wiser hands handle Mercury's energy.

Prepare for June's Ritual

Perform the ritual during daylight on or near either Litha, June 22nd or Father's Day.

~ Seasonings for the Wise Hazel Tree's June Brew ~

For the Ritual Altar~

An Altar Cloth

A Bright Yellow Candle for the Wise Hazel Tree and the Holly King

A Smudge Stick of Sage

A Cauldron to Withstand the Fire's Flame

Herbs, oil and incense for the Potion~ Juniper Berries, Rose, Rosemary, Tangerine, Neroli, Clove, Dragon's Blood, Sandalwood, Amber

Orange Calcite for June's Intent

To Stand Next to A Symbol of Spirit

A Vase of Cut Flowers

A Tree Doll

Your Summer Fun Journal

A Black Currant Scone and a Cool Glass of Orange Spice Tea & a Faery Version for Hazel

Your Wand Made from a Stick

Tasks Before the Ritual

1. Create a nap sachet for under your pillow. Make or buy a little bag to hold tangerine, lemon and mint herbs.

2. Take a break~ as often as you like - for as long as you like, but at least for 20 minutes at a time. Create a restful space that will soothe the senses. Take a nap or rest the eyes. The purpose is twofold~ to relax and make time for your inner child to conjure up some summer fun.

Gently recite this affirmation before resting~

The Child Awaits~

I rest my head on pillowed clouds

with the drifting scent of mint.

Shallow breaths find creeks of dreams

from the quieting touch on my brow.

The Mother protects

caressing my cheeks with the kiss of butterfly lashes.

The door to this world closes snug and sound

as I reach for the child who awaits.

3.   Keep a Summer Fun Journal. When done resting, jot down any delightful insights. It's important not to let your adult self censor the ideas. Then do as many of the fun adventures you can throughout the summer.

4.   Make a list of intentions to nurture the new life of your dreams.

5.   Do some deck, porch, or stoop sitting and watch the clouds go by.

6.   Make or embellish the doll to honor the Wise Hazel Tree.

7.   Select a charm that represents Nurturing New Life and attach it to the wand.

The Day of the Ritual

Prepare the Ritual Feast

A fine bakery makes a good scone. Black currant is chewy and delicious. Brew a cup of Orange Spice Tea with your Moon charged water and cool down over ice. Make a small dish and cup of the same for Hazel, the Tree's Guardian Faery.

Placement of the Altar ~

Lay the altar cloth on the table

For the Four Directions~

Wand in the East

Sage, Herbs, oil and Cauldron in the South

Tea and Scone in the West

Vase of Flowers in the North

In the center of the altar, place the bright yellow candle

for the Wise Hazel Tree and the Holly King

Arrange the symbol for spirit and the Orange Calcite near the yellow candle

Place the Tree doll before the yellow candle

Put your Summer Fun Journal next to the vase of flowers

Set Faery Hazel's treat next to your dish

Scatter trinkets of merriment around the altar

Time to Center and Smudge ~

Cast the Circle ~

Invite the Directions ~

Reader:

Welcome Direction of East, Spirit of Summer Wind. Hot gusts of air blow

across the path. Seek refuge under the trees. His breath is shaded there.

Welcome Direction of South, Spirit of Innocence. Trampoline clouds, jungle

ravines~ magickal make believe. Through fantasy we learn to dream.

Welcome Direction of West, Spirit of Paternal Love. Steady hand, watchful eye, coaching

voice, patient play. Embrace your role on bended knee with open arms for laughs of glee.

(Taste the treat and tea.)

Welcome Direction of North, Spirit of Wisdom. Wise ones tell stories from

beginning to end. Knowing the middle makes all the difference.

Welcome Wise Hazel Tree and Holly King, ruler of the Waning Year.

Come join us this Midsummer day. We seek your protection for

children and crops and the blessing of rays upon dreams.

Light the bright yellow candle.

Bees, Bugs, & Butterflies

A Poem

By the Mother's Helpers~

Reader:

Bees

Bumble, Honey and Diggers

jackets of yellow and black,

stingers in the Mother's Service~

Baskets of pollen,

honeycomb treats,

melted beeswax,

wings on a costume.

Bugs

Lady, June and Lightning

have summer in common.

Wings in the Mother's Service~

Genial guests,

polka dot luck,

metallic green landings,

nightlights in flight.

Butterflies

Monarch, Viceroy and Painted Lady

royalty in company of escort.

Wonder in the Mother's service~

Patterned wings,

beat in slow motion,

light upon hearts,

then wave goodbye.

A Visit to Midsummer Manor

A Solstice Reading

as Told by the Olde Bard, Carolan

Reader:

Hark,

spirits of fun,

birds of summer

awake to the longest day

and travel with me

while the Sun burns bright

to the Manor of the Kings.

Into the woods my heart takes the lead

guided by Wren, my companion.

The path barely open from canopied trees

hitches on the hem of my skirt

filmy and sheer to allow summer's breeze

and the escape of musical notes.

Sewn by Goddesses with child

as they danced around magical flutes.

Farther we go my Wren and I

through meadows of clover

turned red from the Sun overhead.

Stopping to sip from clear crystal streams

and lunch on the fruit of the mulberry.

We rest a spell in the shade of the tree

I in the grass and Wren on a branch,

who keeps watch as he sings me to sleep

Later, we move

into woods deep as dense

until,

the Sun beams a ray not far up ahead.

We follow, trusting the light.

Careful and sure

we walk straight ahead

and into the clearing.

Where the courtly Manor stands glistening

from Midsummer's Sun

and the finish on the newly hung door

as shiny and green as the tree of the King.

Climbing clematis clings to

snaking trellises

one on either side of the door.

Royal purple blooms wind from the ground

and leap from trellis to turret.

Spiraling up to the eye of the point

then, into the wind

signaling the arrival of the victorious King.

A flutter erupts from the wildflowers below

that encircle the Manor and grounds.

Out from the flowers fly hundreds upon hundreds of

butterflies announcing the King.

They swirl and swirl, forming a funnel of wings

in spectacular color and form.

Gathering energy and speed the cone races up

till the leader breaks free of the spin.

The rest burst forth scattering butterfly delight

as they float back down to the earth.

One lands upon me and one on the Wren

stilling our pose like statues on the plaza.

Slowly, we feel a change in the air

as the butterflies return to the wild.

Except, for the Monarchs who line in a row to welcome

their beloved King.

Dressed in a robe of light summer linen

embossed with his signature holly.

The shadow of beard

begins tickling his face.

Along, with the smallest of Monarchs

who jumps from his face to his belly below and onto Baby Doe

whose rustling between her father and King.

An infectious giggle escapes from the doe

starting a rippling of mirth in the stable of eight.

Her father and King nod, marveling at Baby Doe's innocence and wit.

The King turns around taking everything into account.

Once assured that all is well,

his eyes find mine and those of the Wren

and I feel our journey is nearing its end

or beginning, this time they're one and the same.

With Wren on my shoulder, I take the King's hand

that's firm and strong and kind.

We walk towards the door with father and doe in tow

as the Sun crests high in the sky.

The King nudges the doe to the latch in the center

who naturally knows what to do.

Knocking once, faces the wheel to the Moon tide of life

twice, steers the current.

The King whispers thank you to the doe, who whispers the same to her father

completing the waxing phase of the year.

Let the Inauguration Commence,

the Grand Entrance Begin

with

The King,

followed next by

Baby Doe and her father

the Monarchs and deer

and, I with my companion, the Wren.

Carolann Gregoire, MSW

The Festival of Litha

Reader:

Atop the hillside, the Wise Hazel Tree receives the Sun. Her concentration unbreakable, her countenance electric. Leaves shimmer as they hold the light. Air pulsates to a cosmic rhythm. It is Litha. The day the Mother as Tree and the Father as Sun commune.

From Sun up to noon, they consummate their power when she's the most fertile and he's at his zenith. Once a year on this Midsummer's day, they reveal to the other their perspectives on life anew. With branches outstretched, the Tree sees his view from the sky up above. With rays shining down, the Sun senses the earth from the ground below. Understanding unfolds in silent communion. Agreements are reached on what's needed the most. Their decree will be conveyed later this day, by way of the Witch and the Tree.

A large wooden bucket sits beside the resting Tree. Hazel, the Guardian Faery, swoops down filling a small watering can to the very top. The can, whittled from a twig with a petunia shaped spout, was a gift from her friend Coll. Hazel is particularly fond of this gift and uses it only for the most special of occasions, like today, for Litha.

Done with watering the top half of the Tree, Hazel turns her attention to the lower branches. She lands softly on a cluster of leaves and begins to lovingly massage the cool tincture into the veins. "Thank you dear, that feels lovely." The Tree takes a deep breath then remarks, "hmmm, smells good too. What did you and the Witch conjure up this year?" Hazel's hair, which was already standing on end from the static electricity, poofed out even more from the compliment as she said, "The Witch suggested spearmint leaves, mandarin rind and hair of coconut. It's such a hot day, we thought a mix of calming, relaxing and cooling herbs would be best." The Tree smiled and said, "I would agree little Hazel." "The Witch said it was important that you sleep before the ritual so the wisdom can flow into your roots. I added an eensie bit of tonka bean for sweet dreams. I hope that was alright?" asked Hazel. "Indeed it was dear," said the Tree, drifting off into a deep slumber~ smiling. Hazel fusses here and there making sure the Tree sleeps comfortably.

Divine Naked Fire Wiggler, the Witch, can feel the SunTree wisdom making its journey through the Tree's leaves, stems, branches and then trunk. She estimates it will take another hour or so before the decree settles into Her root system. She bends down to add some white sage and another log to the fire. Sweat drips from her swollen belly into the bubbling cauldron. She looks around for her staff and sees it leaning up against the Tree. The chiseled face of her great, great grandfather known as Square Foot, a trapper and surveyor from the Valley of Ontario, looks back in her direction. The staff, his walking stick is imbued with a most helpful property. With the staff in her left hand, Divine Naked Fire Wiggler walks around the sacred circle emitting a steady stream of blue smoke from the staff's wizened lips~ immediately cooling off the space.

She returns to the fire and stirs the cauldron swaying to and fro as she listens to the spirit beat of tribal drums. Divine Naked Fire Wiggler is a much beloved and powerful Witch, guided by her calling and the ancestral blood that pounds in her veins. For most of the year, she travels the valleys birthing and caring for newborns. At Midsummer, the Tree entrusts the Witch to deliver the annual SunTree Decree to the world.

Gauging by the look of the magick, Divine Naked Fire Wiggler takes some Juniper berries out of the pouch hanging from her neck and tosses them into the cauldron turning the brew a rich green. Standing in holy communion with the Tree a hint of pine fills the air and lungs of the Witch. With each breath, the Sun tattoo spreads across her breasts turning the rays a deep shade of the forest, her home. Her hair piled high as a beehive for the brewing is now released, tumbling down to her waist in beautiful dark waves for the ritual. On cue, Hazel removes the Wreath of Daisies hanging from a branch. She places it atop the Witch's head, and settles in beside a daisy as Divine Naked Fire Wiggler turns slowly around to face the Mother's stewards. Quieting the gathering with her presence she begins the dance of her people, the Clan of the Deer.

The Ceremony

Led by Divine Naked Fire Wiggler, the Witch

Reader, follow along with the Witch tossing the herbs, oil and incense into the cauldron.
Reader as the Divine Naked Fire Wiggler:

> *Stewards of the Mother, Children of the Earth,*
>
> *Gather round and listen to the message of the SunTree.*

Early this morn the Tree and the Sun

through transmuted form

pondered in meditation this question~

What does the world need most to nurture life anew?

This is their 6 point Decree~

1

Earth is the eternal feminine.

Draw close to the Mother

let her nourish first

then, may you too.

Reader, toss the essence of Rose into the Cauldron.

2

The planet is feeling the dark night of the soul.

The light is blocked by our fear.

Seek divine counsel,

clarity and calm is assured.

Reader, toss the essence of Rosemary into the Cauldron.

3

The burdens of life are lifted by children's laughter.

Greet the child within.

Resist the posturing of adulthood,

remember the feel of escaping giggles.

Reader, toss the essence of Tangerine into the Cauldron.

4

There is time to reverse the effect of mistakes.

Turn away from the face of destruction.

Look instead to the wise one of the Crone,

envision the world through Her eyes.

Reader, toss the essence of Neroli into the Cauldron.

5

Answers lie outside the box.

Creativity comes from the soul,

enactment joins forces,

limitless possibilities unfold.

Reader, toss the essence of Clove into the Cauldron.

6

Light the fire of purification.

Burn the weeds

choking new growth,

scatter the ashes to feed new life.

Reader, toss the essence of Dragon's Blood into the Cauldron.

The Witch carefully drops a hair from Hazel's head coated in quicksilver into the cauldron. Then she reaches into her pouch and draws out the essence of sandalwood and amber~ the final ingredients needed for the decree's swift, safe and successful journey.

Reader, toss the essence of Sandalwood and Amber into the Cauldron.

Divine Naked Fire Wiggler turns to the Wise Hazel Tree who nods and says, "It is time."

The Witch takes her staff and stirs blue smoke into the cauldron to cool the brew. Hazel gets her watering can. The Witch picks up the wooden bucket. Together they fill them up with ice cold potion all the way to the top. They gently pour the brew over the roots of the Tree. Steam rises encircling the space with aromatic magick. As the Stewards breathe in the sacred air the brew is absorbed through Her roots.

The Wise Hazel Tree feels the SunTree Decree moving through Her and into the Divine Root System that runs underneath the planet. Aided by the potion, their message flows to the living green.

The Wise Hazel Tree asks the stewards to:

Sense the message in

the woodwind's crescendo,

rose scented blooms,

the willow's touch,

dawning light

and,

the taste of the mulberry.

Reader, invite the stewards to read out loud or in silence their intentions for nurturing their dreams' new life. Afterwards, place the lists into the cauldron. Light the potion. Reader, as Divine Naked Fire Wiggler.

Stewards of the SunTree,

I, as the Witch do so decree,

your thoughtful intentions are well received.

Nurture New Life in thought and deed,

Aim to succeed, So Mote It Be!

A Father's Day Blessing

Reader, ask the stewards to bring their Father Figures to mind and then recite:

Father,

May the Moon's tide rock you to sleep

lulling you into sustained slumber.

May you wake each morn

ready to guide the world's children.

May you find joy in your charge,

as you entrust your step in the Mother's lead.

Enjoy the rest of Midsummer's festival. Open the circle

with gratitude for our magickal guests~

The Wise Hazel Tree and Sun

Naked Fire Wiggler, the Witch

Hazel, the Guardian Faery

Coll, the Faun

Holly King

Baby Doe and her Father

The Olde Bard, Carolan

and, the Wren

After the Ritual

Scatter the ashes from the potion at the base of a tree, (If you did March's ritual, use the tree where you planted your dreams.) Put Hazel's treat nearby. Place the Orange Calcite in the Children & Creativity Bagua of the home or room to remember the feel of escaping giggles. Put your Summer Fun Journal in the hub of the home and take as many adventures as you can.

All is Well in the Shade of the Tree

~ Blessed Be ~

Chapter 11

July

Foster Growth

July's Sensual Nature

There is one month each quarter turn that best captures the sensual essence of nature. This is the month among the three where the physical world settles into the rhythm of the season. For summer, it's July when the earth is covered and full, teeming with life. The Sun is hot, the rains still come and gardens and crops continue to mature. The Mother's helpers are busy at work handling nature's demands. Beds of Shasta daisies attract a steady stream of bumble bee suitors reminding us of the instinctual drive to seed a spot in the future. We watch in amazement as flowers grow into vertical beauties. Sunflowers, hollyhocks, tiger lilies and coneflowers are examples of these tall wonders. Their limber stems astound as they sway in the breeze, bend through storms and stand up straight to capture the Sun. The visibility of life in summer form reassures us that all is well in the natural world.

July is neither quiet in sound or spirit. By now, we are accustomed to the whiz of scooters, roar of motorcycles and the whoop and holler of outdoor play. There is much to hear. Porch sitting allows us the opportunity to listen below the hum of the expected, to seek out the flap of wings in puddles, the whirring hover of hummingbirds and the rapid buzz of the cicada. This month, during quiet walks in leafy woods, keep an ear out for the rustling racket of small critters as they forage for supper. Listen for the sudden silence of crickets after one too many steps in their direction.

Even our foods are noisy and messy. Licking our fingers is permissible and necessary. Summer fare is naturally juicy and drippy from just picked berries, burgers with sliced garden tomatoes, fresh grilled corn on the cob brushed in butter and sweet, ripe watermelon. After dinner, our fruit cobblers ooze onto our dessert plates melting the scoop of homemade ice cream. We crunch and munch our way down the garden row~ ours, the neighbors and the farmer's market down the street. There is no mistaking the mouthwatering appeal of fresh fruits and vegetables. Summertime brings out a green appetite in everyone.

It also brings on the heat; that's why water is the element of summer we crave as much as the Sun. There is nothing like the versatility of nature's elixir. The cool, refreshing, life-giving water of the Mother replenishes us from summer's mercury. We need its power to chill. Listening to light rain through an open window immediately synchronizes our breath to the season's laidback cadence. Gentle soakers moisten the soil and nourish the plants. Run off from storms channels into rivers through a myriad of large and small ravines. The creek beds gush for a few days afterwards. The swift current clears out the musty creek smell while dropping off new treasures to be discovered later. Most of the time the world can handle the downpours. Sometimes, it can't. Sometimes, it doesn't rain.

Spiritual customs in part grew from our instinct to survive these examples of nature in Her extreme: hurricanes, floods and droughts. Historically, we accepted that a power greater than ourselves was at play and sought divine counsel and protection. Today, our attempts to control the volatility of mother nature have contributed to the ecological mess we currently face. The challenge of letting nature do Her thing without harmful human intervention is similar to the spiritual theme of the month~ letting our dreams take their own course without too much personal meddling. While we want to identify a wayward turn, the difference between our dreams going off track or taking a different path is not always easy to discern. Sensing the difference is a part of July's spiritual quest.

A Visit to the Wise Hazel Tree

The Sun hangs hot in the sky. With a sigh of relief, the Wise Hazel Tree moves underneath the shade of the Sacred Oak. Together, the Trees begin to adjust their measure of time to the tides of the sea. It has been a year since they last came to the Isle of Avalon. Under the care of the water and Sun, the Trees have returned to replenish their souls. They seek the waves to massage aching roots~ the Sun's rays to keep blight at bay~ and cool, soothing rain to relax heavy branches of green. They flow in sync with the world and each other by following this summer creed~ play as hard as you toil. To the stewards, they are Wise Trees on break from their work. On the Isle of Avalon, they are eternal friends on holiday.

Branches of July's Wise Hazel Tree

Goddess Selene

& the Sea Mothers

Kan~ Career Bagua

Vibration of 7

Sun in Cancer

July resonates within us too as the consummate month of summer. We respond to its look, feel and attitude as if summer is the only season of the year. With school done and gratefully, still one month away we can relax into the luxuriant tempo of summer's muse. Hearts are lighter, minds are carefree and our bodies strut unencumbered by layers of clothes. It's the time for summer vacations. We return to beloved spots and take another week to venture into new terrain. We soak up the Sun, take a break inside and then go back out for more. Thank the Goddess and God we have a month that expects our devotion to pleasure.

This July, visit the Mother's world and allow the neglected parts to stretch and explore while the toiling side takes a brief rest. Our culture works too hard and plays too little. Summer reminds us of that fact. Humans need these intermittent escapes into the mystery of nature. Our desire to exchange the city's exhausting smell with the earthen pull of the countryside comes naturally. Deep within rests an intrinsic connection with the wind and soil. If the economics of long road trips are prohibitive, take day trips instead on scenic byways with the windows rolled down. Look for wildflowers lining the side of the road. Ride on two wheels and feel the release of worries into the wind. Bike into the light dancing through trees overhead. Have lunch in the park and camp out in the backyard. Rest the bones. Have fun whenever, however, and as often as spirit calls.

If possible get to the water. There are many ways to submerge ourselves in this liquid magick, all the way from catching a wave in the deep blue sea to a cool, relaxing bath with candles and music. We each have our preference on how we like our water. The sea offers hot Sun and surf and cabanas filled with coolers, sunscreen and books. Some enjoy lakes and the appeal of docks to push off or jump from. Both offer enticing refreshment. Sometimes, it comes down to the preferred backdrop of our water play: trees and cabins or dunes and beach houses. Whichever tickles your fancy, take advantage of the free flowing spirit of water. Nature does and so do our dreams.

The spirited high jinks of summer carry over into our flower beds and gardens of dreams. Fueled by the Mother's elements and free will, their growth is tangible and at times unmanageable. In our rush to materialize our dreams, we push and prod according to what we think they should be. This tendency is similar to adolescents who in their impatience to grow up, take adult risks without the benefit of the good sense that comes with age. Also, unruly weeds tempt our adolescent desires onto a wayward path just like they do in our gardens. The trick is to prune and coax them into ripeness with an eye to their true path and an ear to divine counsel. Assuming intuition was involved in identifying our dreams, it makes further sense to tap into inner wisdom to clarify the direction of their growth.

Our own counsel can help us decipher the meaning of a goal taking a different course. Two aspects of dream making could be at play. First, internal discord manifesting as flowering weeds may be leading us down the proverbial garden path. Tears from old, dysfunctional scripts could be fertilizing the ground in an effort to maintain the status quo within. This is not to say that we didn't do our work tending the soil to remove impediments beforehand. Sometimes, when forging a new path, another layer of healing is revealed as we begin to experience the new and different fruits of our labor. In this case, internal weeding is needed. A common reservoir for internal discord are the energy centers (chakras) of the body. In meditation and stillness, we can pick up the familiar feel of the weeds. Energy and body work to cleanse and release that which is no longer useful is part of the month's spiritual work. Metaphysical book stores and yoga centers are good places to explore the spiritual/energy resources available in a community.

Secondly, the Mother speaking through our inner voice may have a grander idea than we could ever have imagined. Claiming what we want is a significant first step in a goal's manifestation. In fact, all we need to do initially is identify the 'what'. Unfortunately, we often don't stop there. The Mother has less to work with if we take full responsibility for flushing out the details. The Mother has the vast Universe at her disposal and is therefore much more capable of coming up with how, when, and where. Are we meddling rather than listening? We must pay attention to the results of our efforts. If it feels like we're rolling a boulder up a hill, hitting roadblocks and experiencing increasing frustration with the lack of forward movement, then we're probably meddling. When we listen to the Mother, synchronicity presents us with the how, when and the wherewithal to materialize our desires. The feelings associated with right course of action are usually uplifting and invigorating. We may still encounter challenges as we move with the flow but the current is much more at ease, as are we.

Following our dreams is our spiritual work this month. As good stewards we listen to our inner voice, watch what happens and weed when necessary. This is the serious side of the growing season. The lighter side is having fun, a necessary component to keeping all things in balance. As always, the ancient traditions are here to help. We turn first to Feng Shui and the Career Bagua~ Kan. Influenced by the water element, this Bagua takes us to our own internal deep blue sea. Here we may remember the effects of storms long past, those now raining on our dreams causing weeds to grow. The Sea Goddesses otherwise known as Sea Mothers, dwell within the deep currents of life. They support our remembering and will help us release the chokehold on our dreams.

Astrologically, our Sun kissed sign Cancer is like the shifting tides of the ocean. Cancer is a water sign ruled by the Moon. This is a powerful combination. During adolescence, these dual forces can upset the sensitive temperament of the sign. With support and reassurance the energy matures and settles down. The moody and unruly behavior evens out over time. This is similar to what our dreams are experiencing this month: resistance and maturation. Emotions and intuitive behavior are heavily influenced by the Moon and water. If we can give ourselves up to the energy of Cancer and do our spiritual work under Goddess Selene's moonlit sky, afterwards the Sea Mothers will rock us to sleep in time to the rhythm of the sea.

Rhodonite is the selected stone for July. This intricately veined pink stone reflects Cancer's complex nature and emotional focus. It stimulates the process of healing old hurts particularly trauma wounds and the co-dependent aftermath. Co-dependent behavior, much like weeds, will often distract us from affirming endeavors in an effort to maintain what's known and familiar. Therefore, it's a helpful companion stone while doing inner work. Wearing or carrying the stone during this time will increase the experience of forgiving and forgetting. The stone activates the heart chakra and opens us to a deeper love of self and humanity.

We round out the influence of the ancient traditions with the inclusion of Numerology, the vibration of number seven specifically. As we've seen, fostering the growth of our dreams requires the willingness to do inner work. The energy of seven works with the gentle and supportive nature of Rhodonite to help balance the dark with the light. We invite its company in part because we want to maintain our quotient of fun. We also want to get rid of the weeds without too much arduous pulling. The number seven can help by radiating peace upon our efforts. It also fortifies our faith in ourselves and the Mother to achieve what we have set out to do.

Prepare for July's Ritual

Perform the ritual the night of the Full Moon or within three days before or after.

~ Seasonings for the Wise Hazel Tree's July Brew ~

For the Ritual Altar~

An Altar Cloth

A Silver Candle for Goddess Selene and Father Sky

A Smudge Stick of Sage

A Bowl to Withstand the Fire's Flames

Rhodonite for July's Intent

To Stand Next to a Symbol of Spirit

A Bowl of Water with Floating Candles

Netting and Silver Ribbon

A Selene Doll

A List of Weeds

Dish of Berry Cobbler with Ice Cream and a Glass of Ice Cold Water with a Slice of Lemon

Seashells Scattered About to Welcome the Sea Mothers

Your Wand Made From a Stick

Tasks Before the Ritual

1. Select a dream in which you have put recent effort. Examine the current results. Identify any emotional or thought clogged weeds impeding your dream's growth. Take baths or showers if needed and allow the water to raise the weeds to the surface. Take as much time as you need up until the night of the ritual. When you have completed your review, make a list of the weeds you wish to pull.

Recite this prayer to help pick them.

Goddess Selene, Nurturing Mother,

Settle my nerves

my fear of inner depths.

Wrap me in protective arms as I

drain the reservoir of pain clogging my dreams.

Let rise to the surface

those weeds whose time for pulling have come.

I trust my journey is safe in your keep.

2.   Buy a foot of netting and silver ribbon.

3.   Go on vacation! Or, take day trips! Or, do both.

4.   Play in water. Listen to water.

5.   Make or embellish a doll to honor Selene, Goddess of the Full Moon.

6.   Have a cookout or picnic and plan the menu around seven finger-licking foods.

7.   Select a charm that represents Fostering Growth and attach it to the wand.

The Day of the Ritual

Prepare the Ritual Feast

Make or buy a berry cobbler. Serve it up with ice cream and

a tall glass of ice water with a slice of lemon.

Placement of the Altar ~

Lay the altar cloth on the table

For the Four Directions~

Wand in the East

Sage and Burning Bowl in the South

Bowl of Water and Floating Candles in the West

Pie and Ice Water with Lemon in the North

In the center of the altar, place the silver candle for Goddess Selene and Father Sky

Arrange the symbol for spirit and the Rhodonite near the silver candle

Place the Selene doll before the candle

Lay the List of Weeds and netting next to the bowl of water

Scatter the seashells about the altar to honor the Sea Mothers

Time to Center and Smudge ~

Cast the Circle ~

Invite the Directions ~

Reader:

Welcome Direction of East, Spirit of Flow. Smooth, rolling, streams of dreams.
Over, under, around we go. Past sticks, rocks and muddy dams.

Welcome Direction of South, Spirit of Frivolity. Sunny inspiration~ unexpected treasure.
Daylight rains down from the sky, filling moonlit puddles with flecks of gold.

Welcome Direction of West, Spirit of Summer Flavor. Lemonade~ the drink of fairs
and Sunday picnics. Thirst quenching, lemon scented gulps of tart, icy, sweet yellow.
(Have a bite of berry pie and sip of icy lemon water.)

Welcome Direction of North, Spirit of Fullness. The river runs
with the Earth. The sea swims with the Moon. The lake dances
with the Sun. Each full and on course with the Mother.

Welcome Goddess Selene and Father Sky. Goddess Selene rest easily against
the Father's Night Sky as you wait for the call of the Sea Mothers.
Light the silver candle.

The Gossamer Net

A Tale

Spun by Morgan Le Fey, Sea Goddess of the British Isles

Reader as Morgan Le Fey:

One night, under the light of the full Moon I caught a glimpse of a gossamer net just past
the shoreline off the Isle of Avalon. It was hanging just above the water's surface with no
visible means of support. It moved as the sea moved, undulating back and forth. A moonbeam
caught in the floating net bounced upon lace spun from sterling threads. After a few moments,
it landed in the center and promptly melted, spreading across the net's silvery fiber. The
shimmering effect allowed me to see what was hidden before. Dangling from each of the net's
seven rounded points were jewels from the land and sea.

Tempted by their beauty, I walked into the sea and out towards the net. I circled it once, then twice wondering if I should touch the hanging baubles. I decided as Mistress of Avalon, the isle of restorative powers, it was my duty to explore this treasure. I meant no harm I reasoned. But, truth be told I simply could not resist the net's charm.

And, so began a most wondrous night. I closed my eyes to sense the inner mystery patterned in the net and placement of the jewels. A gentle voice said, "The gems must be touched in order of the chakras; find the first." I was pulled to the Coral's red branches and immediately felt a warm sensation deep in my loins. As I held it, the face of a woman appeared. I listened to her story and those of the other Sea Mothers as I held their energy talismans in turn.

~

"I am Sedna, Goddess of Sea Mammals.
An Eskimo first, I once lived upon the land, but now I rule the deepest part of the sea.
I represent the part of the self most feared.
Come to me, I will show you the way out of chaos.
I will ensure a safe and protected journey."

~

I felt a drawing in around my navel as next I touched the Fire Opal.
The face of Fand, an Irish Sea Goddess, appeared.
"I am schooled in the old ways of healing, and serve the Mother on the Emerald Isle.
My place is to remind Her stewards that personal power is gender free.
Come to me to release deep-seated pain inflicted by others.
My lullaby will keep you safe."

~

As I held the Amber I felt the Sun radiate around my belly.
The face of Oshun, an African Sea River Goddess, appeared.
"My love for you is as fierce as the river's current.
I can teach you how to care for the self.
Let me rock you while you experience the depth of your love."

~

My heart swelled when next I touched the Chrysoprase.

The face of Mor, Queen of the Island of Women, appeared.

"I am a Celtic Sea Goddess, a Keeper of the Mysteries.

Tell the truth, at least to the self,

for the mysteries dwell within an honest heart.

My embrace will ease the release of deception."

~

As soon as I held the Aquamarine, my voice rang true.

The face of Mari, the Mermaid, appeared.

"I am the Mediterranean Mother of the Sea.

Speak your sorrows or risk drowning in them.

May this stone of courage brace you against the forces of darkness."

~

Touching the Azurite caused a swooning sensation in my brow.

The beautiful face of Thetis, the Nymph, appeared.

"I am a Greek Sea Goddess, the calmer of stormy seas.

Wipe the heavy mist from your vision.

I will hold the course till you can see for yourself."

~

Purple rays of Amethyst entered my crown as I reached for the stone

The face of Stella Maris, the Roman Goddess of the Sea, appeared.

"I am the Star of the Sea. I walk on the water as my son once did.

It is possible to come to terms with tremendous loss.

Allow the cleansing powers of Amethyst to wash away your tears.

The Light and Love of All There Is will take grief's place."

~

When I had encircled the net I noticed one last gem nestled in the

center. A creamy, iridescent Pearl, the Crown Jewel of the Sea.

The face of Selene, a Full Moon Goddess, appeared

as her gentle voice said, "The pearl is a catalyst for change.

Beauty may be polished from the roughest of edges.

The Goddesses of the Moon and Sea have chosen you,

Morgan Le Fey, as keeper of the Gossamer Net.

This is our gift to you and those who walk the path with the Great Mother.

Under a full Moon, those seeking healing may toss their woes onto the

net. Thereby entrusting their release to the Mothers of the Sea.

Walk in Peace ~ Blessed Be"

Toss the Weeds

A Banishing Spell

Led by Morgan Le Fey

Reader, Invite the stewards to place their list of weeds in their lap and close their eyes. Recite as Morgan Le Fey:

Imagine the beach on the Isle of Avalon. Feet touching the water's edge. Sand

rubbing between your toes. The gentle lapping of water around your ankles.

Dunes watching your back. It is safe to welcome the sea. Take in the damp air,

taste of salt and the sound of the surf. Feel the alchemy at work. The power of the

Mother's ocean. Breathe deep. Again. Time your breath with the rolling waves.

Pull the sea in, Push the sea out. Align your current with the Waters of Life.

Look out from the shore to the stillness beyond the waves' crest where the Moon's

reflection illumines. Watch the Gossamer Net break free of the surface and follow

the ripple of jeweled droplets as it widens into a protective circle. Observe as one

by one the Sea Mothers rise next to their talisman representing their chakra:

Sedna~ the root, Fand~ the navel, Oshun~ the solar plexus, Mor~ the

heart, Mari~ the throat, Thetis~ the third eye, and Stella Maris~ the

crown. Each holds the net where their talisman rests~ honoring the

promise made by them and Goddess Selene to me, Morgan Le Fey.

Reader, hold the ritual net and instruct the stewards to open their eyes and hold their weeds in their hands. Give everyone an opportunity to read their list out loud or in silence. After each steward reads the list, toss the weeds into the net. If there were particular chakras choked by the weeds, the steward may call out the name of the corresponding Sea Mothers and repeat:

Sea Mothers, I willingly toss these weeds into the Gossamer Net

entrusting them into your care. Do what ye will. So Mote it Be.

Reader, when everyone has tossed their weeds into the net, tie it with the silver ribbon and hold it while you recite as the Sea Mothers:

Stewards, your desire to further your dreams is confirmed by the courage

you have shown the days of this month and again this night. Your trust is not

misplaced. We the Mothers of the Sea, willingly accept the pain pulled from your

depths now tossed onto the net. The alchemy of this night will transmute your

sorrow into food for the creatures of the Sea. Make way for the dreams.

So Mote it Be

Goddess Selene's Blessing

Reader, instruct the stewards to close their eyes again and recite as Morgan Le Fey:

The Moon full and bright watches the Sea Mothers as the Net slowly descends

back under the Sea. The Goddesses silently form a crescent Moon in the water~

points facing away from the shore. Their eyes turn to gaze at the Moon just as a

tapestry of moonbeams unrolls from the sky and stops before the crescent.

In a wing's beat, a horse drawn chariot carrying the Goddess Selene glides down

the moonbeams, landing softly in front of the Sea Mothers. Selene, in sterling robes

stands showing the full measure of the Goddess. The Moon's light shines through

gossamer wings. A silver crescent Moon with points facing skyward adorns a golden

crown. With arms outstretched, palms posed to release her power, the kind and

nurturing Goddess imbued with powers of manifestation and healing begins.

Reader as Goddess Selene:

Good stewards, welcome this full Moon night to the Isle of Avalon. I have observed

from above your bravery through the dark night of the soul. Your dreams must be

just and true to have journeyed this far. You have taken care to plant them in good

soil, tend to their early growth and remove the weeds directing their path.

You have done well my stewards. You have my blessing. Moonbeams released from her

hands land gently upon the crown chakras of her stewards. As I leave you this night remember to call upon me and the Mothers of the Sea when in doubt of your course, flow with the Moon's tide and believe that your dreams are but a wing's beat from certainty.

Reader resume as Morgan Le Fey:

Eyes follow as Goddess Selene carried by her fair stallion lands safely back home~ Keeping watch till the chariot's silhouette slips behind the Moon.

Enjoy the feast! Open the circle with gratitude for our divine guests~

Selene, Goddess of the Full Moon

Father Sky

Morgan Le Fey, Sea Goddess of the British Isles

&

the Other Sea Mothers~

Sedna, Goddess of Sea Mammals

Fand, Irish Sea Goddess

Oshun, African River Sea Goddess

Mor, Queen of the Island of Women

Mari the Mermaid, Mediterranean Mother of the Sea

Thetis the Nymph, Greek Sea Goddess

Stella Maris, Star of the Sea and Roman Goddess of the Sea

<u>After the Ritual</u>

Ask for a volunteer to toss the net of weeds into a body of water within three days of the full Moon. A creek, stream, lake, river or sea will do. Remove the weeds from the net before you toss them in so little water creatures aren't snagged. Place your Rhodonite in the Career Bagua of the home or room as a loving reminder of your courage. Return to the water when you feel the pull of familiar weeds. Allow the Sea Mothers to guide your dream's unfolding.

All is Well in the Shade of the Tree

~ Blessed Be ~

Chapter 12

August
Prepare to Harvest

Carolann Gregoire, MSW

August's Sensual Nature

We have reached the dog days of summer. July was hot, but August is hotter still. The rains don't soak the ground as often leaving the earth a little dusty. The water that almost overflowed the banks last month now meanders down the middle of drying creek beds. Baked by the Sun, nature begins to lose a little of its shiny luster. Leaves, still abundant, begin to curl inward from lack of moisture. Coneflowers bleached by the Sun fade in color; their seeds are now food for yellow finches. Green lawns once barefoot soft are now mixed with patches of scratchy brown.

August is a month of mixed sensations. While it remains beautiful and colorful, it no longer resonates the pure essence of summer. The carefree veneer of early summer cracks under the heat revealing the growing season's final layer of purpose, harvesting. The shift is subtle at first while cookouts and campouts occupy us. Midway through the month we become more aware of earth's readiness for harvest, specifically Her cereal crops. Drives down country roads display row upon row of stalks heavy with corn swaying in the hot breeze. Nature's timing coincides with advertisements reminding us to get our children ready for school. Harvesting and back to school preparations lather a thick coat of responsibility onto summer's fun surface. This is part of the circle of life. If we infused the rest of the year with the playful attitude of the season, we might not mourn its ending as much.

Although the temperature suggests otherwise, August does begin the slip into fall. It carries the distinction of being the first of three harvest months even though, harvesting is associated primarily with the season of autumn. That is why some who prefer hot sunny days begin to droop a little just like some late summer flowers. We may wilt under the orange August Sun, but not the grain crops. The moisture needed for growing is not welcomed when it comes time to harvest. The parent plants and seeds must be dry to help prevent spoilage afterwards. The delicate balance between temperature, Sun and water is especially important for the Mother to maintain during harvest.

Cereal crops are a global and sacred staple. Of the crops produced, maize, rice and wheat give the highest yield. Although other nutrients are present, it is the starch and fiber we crave because it tastes good and is filling. A bowl of oatmeal in the morning with brown sugar and butter lasts us until lunch. Interestingly, there are more benefits to starch than strictly dietary. In fact, corn starch is used primarily in non-food products like paper, adhesives, binders, fillers, plastics and fuel alcohol. Maize or corn is the primary source of these commercial uses of starch. Clearly, grains are a significant natural commodity for the world's food supply and everyday products. It's no wonder that this month's Sabbat, Lughnasadh, is also known as the cereal harvest. The holiday demonstrates the importance ancient pagans placed on honoring and nurturing the Mother's grain. The changing climate and subsequent water shortages affecting current grain production around the globe, only heightens the relevance of this Sabbat in today's world.

A Visit to the Wise Hazel Tree

The smell of baking bread was drawing a small crowd up the hill where the steward was busy kneading another loaf of Eight Grain Goddess Bread. The earth oven fired up since dawn had already turned out multiple loaves for the festival of Lughnasadh later in the day. Seeing their appetites grow as they made their way up, the Wise Hazel Tree turned to Goddess Ceres and said, "Dear, why don't you tear up those practice loaves from this morning and pass them out to the villagers. I don't like to see hungry faces on my children. The steward should have plenty of bread ready in time for the harvest celebration."

Branches of August's Wise Hazel Tree

Lughnasadh~ Cereal Harvest

Li~ Fame & Reputation Bagua

Vibration of 8

Sun in Leo

Lughnasadh is a hearty festival full of blessings of gratitude and hopeful prayers for the rest of the harvest season. Edain McCoy tells us Lughnasadh derives its name from the Irish Sun God Lugh. This God is responsible for shining his light filled rays upon the fields during the growing season between the Spring and Autumn Equinoxes. The festival, also known as Lammas, celebrates the fruits of the first harvest and Lugh's role in ensuring abundant crops. He is a giving God and influences the holiday's altruistic focus on sharing the bounty. This generosity also acknowledges the continuation of the growing season and the circle of life. We're born, live and give back to the earth. The reciprocity of giving and receiving is as natural as the in and out flow of breath. The old custom of throwing grains, particularly corn back into the field symbolizes the necessity of guaranteeing future crops. The Goddess representing the circle of life remains pregnant this month while she helps the Sun care for the earth's new yield.

Throughout the winter, spring, and summer, we have discovered and nurtured our bliss-filled dreams. We have listened to our inner voice and sought the counsel of the wise ones. Some tending will be necessary, but our responsibility now is to let them grow as nature intends. Our months of effort will ensure their fulfillment, for we have been present from our dream's first inception and its rise like a swelling womb. We have steadied its first steps to keep the dream on course. It is time for our dreams to grow with careful abandon as they flourish under the Sun's watch. And, if like young adults, they need to come back home for some 'lovin from the oven' we will be there to encourage and support our dreams realization. With the help of God Lugh, we too will have a successful harvest.

Although any month we can feel the warmth of the Sun is a good month, there is something special about the star's reign in August. Under its influence, the month vibes a yellow-orange energy thus setting the stage for fall's amber mood. We soak up the Sun's color hoping but knowing it won't last us through the winter. We appreciate the Sun differently in August because it foretells the end of a beloved season. There are other holidays that honor our star but none captures its essence quite like Lughnasadh. During this harvest celebration, the Sun is exalted as we experience the Sun's power to create life. His command is understood. His reign is unequaled. And, for this, we are grateful beyond measure.

Leo is literally the Sun kissed sign of the month. Leo energy is strong, magnetic and exuberant. It rises to match the Sun's power and basks in its glory. If arrogant at times, so be it. It is both a blessing and a burden to carry the heat of the Sun. When harnessed, Leo energy can manifest anything. Leos are natural leaders with incredible willpower. When channeled for the good of all, great things can happen for humanity. When misused, the energy can become entitled and self-serving. Leo's loyalty and generosity offset the exacting expectations of self and others. The energy of the Sun through Leo is perfect for the initial harvest of our dreams. Leo's mantra, it will be done, appropriately states our expectations.

Tiger's eye, our stone for August, is beautiful like the energy it complements. Yellow Tiger's Eye is earthen in color polished in the shiny luster of the Sun. The dark and rich striated colors seem to shift when held under light, giving it a magickal luminescence. It's both lovely and helpful. As an abundance stone for Leo, it acts as a dream catalyst for us. Its combined energies of the earth and Sun give the stone its manifestation qualities. The stone constructively directs the sign's willful energy keeping it on a benevolent path. The energy gravitates to highly principled enterprises which lends a measure of integrity to Leo's creative exploits. Furthermore, Tiger's Eye can help clarify the intention and direction of a goal.

At this stage, our dreams are visible and palpable. The energy of the Fame & Reputation Bagua~ Li can foster their maturity for their harvest. This Bagua's energy focuses on the external associations we develop as we build our dreams. Our reputation matters. Philosophically, honest and fair personal and business dealings foster wealth and abundance for those involved. Generosity of spirit and deed ensures our success and the success of others. This is the intention of the Bagua. When power is involved, resolve can falter. This Bagua can help temper Leo's leaning toward self-aggrandizement and the potential spillover onto the ground of our dreams. The Bagua reminds us that the best outcome of our hard earned success enlivens others as well.

Numerologically, the vibration of eight is a remarkable fit with this month's theme. Eight's energy is strong and achievement oriented. It brings to the harvest a thorough and dependable work ethic, a follow through spirit to the end if you will. Our dreams are ready. We can trust they'll master the fine points of maturity with experience. The gifts of the ancient traditions this month all point to one thing, success.

Prepare for August's Ritual

Perform the ritual on the first or second of the month at

Lughnasadh or, before Leo's full Moon.

~ Seasonings for the Wise Hazel Tree's August Brew ~

For the Ritual Altar~

An Altar Cloth

A Sunny Orange Candle for God Lugh and Goddess Ceres

A Smudge Stick of Sage

A Bowl to Withstand the Fire's Flames

Tiger's Eye for Augusts' Intent

To Stand Next to a Symbol of Spirit

Your Dream in Flight Reflection

A Bread Basket

A Bowl of Corn

A Ceres Doll

A Hearty Slice of Artisan Bread and a Tall Glass of Summer Blend Tea

Your Wand Made from a Stick

Tasks Before the Ritual

1. Select a dream ready for harvest. In quiet solitude, ponder its inception and growth. Consider the twists and turns of its path. See the dream as it stands today. Write on a piece of paper a brief summary of your reflection and label it *Dream in Flight*.

2. For the month of August, visit fruit stands and farmer's markets for your produce.

3. If you have a garden, continue sharing your vegetables with friends and neighbors.

4. Make homemade or buy artisan bread from local bakers and brew a summer blend tea from your Moon charged water.

5. Clean out closets of unused clothing and make a donation to a local charity.

6. Donate food to a community food pantry.

7. Make or embellish a Ceres doll. Traditionally, the doll is pregnant this month.

8. Soak up the Sun while it lasts & Enjoy the rest of summer!

9. Select a charm to symbolize your dream's preparation for harvest and attach it to the wand.

The Day of the Ritual

Prepare the Ritual Feast ~

Cut thick slices of bread and put them in your basket for the altar.

Keep one slice for the treat alongside the glass of tea.

Placement of the Altar ~

Lay the altar cloth on the table

For the Four Directions ~

Wand in the East

Burning Bowl in the South

Bread and Drink in the West

Basket of Bread & Bowl of Corn in the North

In the center of the altar, place the sunny orange candle for God Lugh and Goddess Ceres

Arrange the symbol for spirit and the Tiger's Eye near the sunny candle

Place the Ceres doll before the candle

Lay the Dream in Flight Reflection next to the basket of bread

Scatter the altar with Sun symbols

Time to Center and Smudge ~

Cast the Circle ~

Invite the Directions ~

Reader:

Welcome Direction of East, Spirit of Summer's Essence. Mourn
not summer's close. Relish the dog days. File away memories made
with loved ones under the Sun~ for fireside reminiscing.

Welcome Direction of South, Spirit of Careful Abandon. Young dreams hot to the touch
cool under the shade of the Wise Hazel Tree. In Her care, pliable dreams meld into reality.

Welcome Direction of West, Spirit of Pride. Leo's roar fires dreams
into flight. Inhale the sweet after breath of success.
(Have a bite of bread and drink of tea.)

Welcome Direction of North, Spirit of Community. Share the harvest in the Mother's
name. Reach out to those in need of food and light. As we give so shall we receive.

Welcome God Lugh and Ceres, Roman Goddess of Corn. Your blessings have raised
our crops to bounty heights. We thank you for sunlight and fertile soil. To ensure a good
yield, we ask that your blessings continue through the rest of the harvest season.

Light the sunny orange candle.

Dawn's Rise

A Summer Poem

Inspired by the Mother's Leo

Reader:

Eyes open to dark night

Then, close again till morning light.

Outside images impose

on lids shut tight.

Deep slumber turns to fitful doze.

Morning intrudes unwelcomed at first

as thoughts of the day rush in.

The mind begins

a litany of commands

in jumbled and tumbled bursts.

Breathe in, breathe out, to quiet the mind.

Relinquish control,

lay still,

drink in dawn's rise

till mind and body have tasted their fill.

Eyes open to sunlight

and greet the Mother's day.

Cicadas sleep to the lark's morning song

as summer's breeze slips under the sheets

bringing a hint of August's bouquet.

Dawn's Rise,

quiet and gentle,

brings peace to mind and body.

Loving and soft it

soothes a restless heart,

allowing spirit to lead

us forth into day.

The Steward's Journey

A Reading

Reflections With the Wise Hazel Tree

Reader as the Wise Hazel Tree:

Come here steward, sit beside me under the shade. Your dream's journey is now almost complete. I remember the day you found me and the rejoining of our spirits. The longing in your eyes told me you had been searching for years for the ground upon which to grow your seeds of service. You seemed surprised that the hope and trust you placed in spirit to lead you here had finally come true. I remember you told me it was the most indescribable sense of knowing you had ever experienced. Sheer bliss overtook you that day and has stayed with you hence as you've learned and served the Mother well.

The journey of a steward is spirit's manifestation on earth. It is a repeating cycle of learning, leading and following the wheel of life around and again. The closer we live with Mother Earth the clearer our role and purpose becomes. It is a humbling experience to live in step with nature, to feel our unique rhythm beat alongside the pulse of the universe. It is not an easy path, to really love the self and others. Nor, is it easy to trust that all is well and will be in the midst of chaos, particularly in times when our spiritual potential outmatches our human abilities. And, when our religious differences seem so insurmountable.

But, as a wise priest once said, "There are many paths to spirit." "Steward, you have chosen the way of the olde religion. Other stewards will choose another. We all call earth our home. On this we can agree. And, it is from this most basic, undeniable fact that hope for our world resides. The Song of Spirit has many melodies. We must listen beyond the lyrics to discover the music common to us all. I respect your willingness to listen to spirit's song. There will be time in the harvest months to come for reflection on the wisdom gained from your dream's realization to serve. But for now, Rejoice as your Dream Takes Flight."

The Ceremony of Lughnasadh

Led by the Steward,

the Sun God, Lugh & Ceres, the Goddess of Corn

Reader, hold the basket of bread and recite as the Steward:

God Lugh and Goddess Ceres,

Powers of Sun & Earth

Welcome to our Lammas Celebration.

We've felt the Sun's steadying beat, readying our dreams for flight

as fields give up their grain

We've toiled then rested under havens of shade

as rivers became currents of sustenance.

Powers of Sun & Earth,

The land stands full

beautiful in bounty,

a Grateful sight to the Mother's children.

We the Stewards

are ready to harvest the Mother's crops.

Her Grains & Our Dreams

both intertwined

in the growing cycle of life.

We share this bread with each other and the Powers of Sun & Earth

in humble gratitude for our journey together.

Reader, pass the bread and enjoy the sharing of harvest grain.

Reader, hold the bowl of corn and continue as Goddess Ceres:

Stewards,

The land gives, so shall we.

I accept your offering and return in kind

a scattering of corn across the fields.

Each kernel blessed by me will take root in the Mother's soil.

Reader, scatter some of the corn across the altar and resume as Goddess Ceres:

Stewards,

What have you to offer the Mother?

Reader, pass the bowl of corn around the group. Encourage the stewards to toss a kernel of corn onto the altar as they share how they gave back to the community this month.

Reader continue as Goddess Ceres:

Your deeds will grow in measure of the love shown to your

brethren. I am pleased by your generosity.

Reader, ask the stewards to hold their *Dream in Flight* reflections and continue as God Lugh:

Stewards,

My rule that lasts from spring's to autumn's equinox is but half of the year.

Yet, there is much to accomplish in the Mother's growing time.

The land of dreams and crops must be readied for planting, the soil

and new shoots tended, and the early growth nurtured.

It is a journey unachievable without each other,

for without your hands my rays fall on fallow ground

and without my Sun your seeds are stilled by darkness.

Lughnasadh is a celebration of Divine Unity

between the Heavens and Earth

and the bridge in between.

As you honor the Sun & Earth this day,

we honor you, our stewards, the bridge in between.

It is time to release your Dreams into Flight.

Stewards, call your dreams out loud as my rays light them into flight.

Behold the sunlight of creation burst forth from the Mother's womb.

So Mote it Be!

Reader, invite the stewards to read their *Dream in Flight* reflections and light them into flight by the sunny orange candle's flame.

Enjoy the Lammas feast! Open the circle after expressing

thanks to our distinguished guests~

Sun God Lugh

Ceres, Roman Goddess of Corn

The Mother's Leo

The Wise Hazel Tree

& you, Her Stewards

<u>After the Ritual</u>

Divide the corn from the altar among the stewards. Scatter the kernels in gardens and fields to help ensure a bountiful harvest. Place your Tiger's Eye in the Fame & Reputation Bagua of the home or room to bless your Dream in Flight and recite this final blessing~

Hidden Bliss, Discovered Desire, Nurtured Goal.

Now Dream in Flight,

Soar to Sights Unknown.

Born of the Sun & Earth, Fly at Your Will

To Destinies Yet to Be!

All is Well Under the Shade of the Tree

~ Blessed Be ~

Appendix

Guide for Ritual Making

Guide for Ritual Making

(A general approach for ritual preparation and tool making)

To accomplish the intention of living and dreaming more compatibly with the natural world, each ritual reflects the sensual and spiritual purpose of the season and the month in which it falls. Amazingly, but not surprisingly, the spiritual themes take their cue from Mother Nature quite effortlessly. What will be asked of you personally each month expands your connection to your inner spirit and the earth. There is a natural flow between the season, its three months and one season to the next. The timing of the rituals is based on lunar cycles for magick making and Wiccan holidays. It's important to center the ritual around the time when the energy is the most conducive to the purpose at hand.

Each ritual contains common elements that will be reviewed in this guide. Generally, there are tasks to be performed prior to and the day of the ritual in preparation of the ceremony. The tasks and ritual itself are designed to accomplish the intention without becoming burdensome. For instance, walking is a central task to ritual preparation. Quiet, solitary walks in the woods and neighborhood enlivens the senses and increases your awareness of each month's natural offerings. Some rituals are longer with more spells because of the sensual and spiritual nature of the month. The ceremony may be performed alone or in a group. Certain months lend themselves to a gathering of like minded folks such as All Hallow's Eve and May Day. When a group is involved, the leadership roles should be assigned ahead of time. Assignments should reflect the strengths and willingness of the participating stewards.

The general outline for performing a ritual is as follows~

Make the Ritual Feast

Placement of the Altar

Center and Smudge

Cast the Circle

Invite the Directions

Readings

Magick Making~ Spells and Incantations

Enjoy the Feast

206

Open the Circle

And, if you wish, an occasional daily affirmation for the rest of the month

In more detail~

1. Making the Ritual Feast~ each month a simple drink and treat will be served on the altar for the stewards in attendance. The feast is an offering to spirit and for your enjoyment.

2. Placement of the Altar~ Locate a sacred space that may be used for the rituals. The space should be clutter free, aesthetically pleasing and quiet. The items on the altar will reflect the colors and intention of a given ritual but will generally include these core elements~

An altar cloth of your choosing. If you wish, change the cloth to fit the ritual.

Candles to symbolize Mother Earth, and Father Sky

Symbols and candles for the four directions

Symbols for spirit and the monthly intent

a Cauldron or burning bowl

a Goddess Doll

Sage

a Wand

Readings

Spell making tools

Items selected for your own merriment

Traditionally in February we begin using a Goddess doll. The Sabbat of Imbolc introduces the concept of making a doll from husks, stalks and other bits of nature leftover from the last harvest. You may also create the doll in whatever manner you desire. Whichever month you begin the book, you may introduce the Goddess doll. The doll will reflect the particular theme of the month.

3. Center and Smudge~ a centering and smudging exercise begins each ritual. Select ahead of time a simple centering meditation that compliments your style of releasing the day's business and going within. Smudging is a Native American practice used to remove negative energy from the space and the persons present. It is important to be present in body and spirit when directing the Mother's energy for ritual intent. Your method of choice is used to center and

ground your chi or energy in the now. If there are stewards in attendance new to ritual, the following poem may be read before the smudging process.

Take the time you need to set yourself free from niggling reminders of things yet to do.

Allow for time and space to join with the source

and receive spirit's grace.

Once centered and still, use the sage to remove any lingering and unhelpful residue.

Used as a stick or loose it matters not~

to the energy it cleanses within and without.

Draw the smoke to the self and wash your face free

of the mask that is worn for others to see.

Let it waft and swirl over you and the room,

leaving that which is needed to begin anew.

Feeling present and grounded the Mother decrees,

the ritual is upon us ~

Blessed Be.

4. Casting the Circle~ the wand is a tool used to create a sacred and protected space in which to perform the ceremony. It allows for a free, uninhibited, safe space to fully participate in the ritual experience. This poem is instructive for readers unfamiliar with casting the circle.

Envision the Mother with your wand held aloft.

Feel the intake of breath as you draw from the Moon.

Into the wand flows the Moon's silver glow,

the nectar of the Mother will protect us from others.

Hold the wand in your left hand and out to the side.

Now release her protection in a strand of silver light.

Walk the compass beginning and ending with east.

Once around is enough to encircle in peace.

With your eyes and wand skyward,

send back to the Moon

the last of the light,

thanking the Mother for protection this nite.

5. Inviting the Four Directions~ Wiccan ceremonies acknowledge the spiritual nature of earth by welcoming the elemental spirits of east, south, west, and north. The invitation is extended through verse and symbols placed directionally on the altar. Each ritual will contain verse and symbols specific to the month's intention, but will also include the general energy of each direction. Candles may be used for each direction in addition to these symbols. The candle is lit after the invitation to the specific direction is made.

East~ spirit of air, energy of the mind

South~ spirit of fire, energy of creation

West~ spirit of water, energy of the heart

North~ spirit of earth, grounding energy of the Mother

Mother Earth ~ Yin, the divine feminine and

Father Sky ~ Yang, the divine masculine

6. Readings~ Readings have been composed to honor the seasonal and spiritual essence of each month. Stewards are invited to include additional readings meaningful to them.

7. Magick Making~ Spells and Incantations~ This is light magick performed for our good. The ritual spells are intended to help us live and dream seasonally and achieve specific goals. At times, the spells will be the completion of a task the steward began earlier in the month. Other spells of your choice may be included. Some of the rituals will include divination. Divination is a method of communication between your higher self and your conscious self. We each have the ability to intuit this information although, some are more naturally in touch with this sixth sense. Divination tools include: message decks and cards such as tarot, faery, animal totem, and Goddess, the I Ching, and rune toss, and other forms such as pendulums, palm reading, and scrying. Generally, we seek information to answer a puzzling question, validate a hunch or path, seek resolution to a problem, or point us in the right direction. An intuitive many years ago offered this sound advice regarding divination: the information is not absolute and should be approached as a probable outcome if the course of action we've chosen remains unchanged. This perspective allows us to receive information to help us maintain or change the course. If you are not familiar with the concept, visit a metaphysical bookstore

and peruse the divination section. If this is your cup of tea, the right divination method will find you.

8. Enjoy the Feast~ Feast and make merry. Each ritual contains a suggested menu, simple and tasty.

9. Open the Circle~ When the ceremony is complete, offer thanks to the spirits and invited guests and blow out the candles. The steward who cast the circle may now release it by drawing the light back into the wand while walking counterclockwise beginning and ending with east. Once around, release the light back to the Moon.

10. 10. Daily Affirmation~ In some months, a simple daily affirmation is included with the ritual. The affirmation serves as a reminder to center our lives on the offerings of the month. The suggested ritual candle may be used for the affirmation. You may blow the candle out after the meditation or allow it to burn for 30 minutes. If needed, additional candles may be used. The first time you recite the affirmation the candle becomes charged with the intent.

Tool Making

Two general tools will be needed for the rituals~ a wand and charged water.

1. The wand will evolve over the course of the twelve rituals and begins with the selection of a sturdy and thick stick. Each month a small charm signifying the ritual intent will be selected by the steward and attached to the wand. Select beads and charms that may be attached by wire, glue, twine or by other simple means.

2. The Full Moon is the best phase in which to charge water. The night of the moonrise pour a half a quart of filtered or spring water into a glass or ceramic basin and place outside. Select an elevated and secure place such as a chair or table on the deck or porch. Allow twenty-four hours for the water to be fully charged. Store the water in an airtight container at room temperature. To brew the beverage of choice in the rituals, use about a tablespoon of charged water per cup.

Glossary

The Use of Ancient Traditions in Ritual

The Use of Ancient Traditions in Ritual

(Astrology, Numerology, Feng Shui and Wicca)

Astrology~ Influence of the Sun Sign

The aspect of Astrology we understand best is the influence of the Sun sign on a person's life journey. Our temperament and inclination toward all manner of things are due in part to a singular event, our birthday. The energy expressed through a Sun sign is shaped by that sign's governing planet. It is this planet which helps explain its inherent strengths, challenges and influence. When the Sun lights upon our sign, we certainly bask in its celebratory rays throughout our birthday month. We also react to the Sun's changing energy, birthday or not, and often times, unknowingly.

Each month two Sun signs reign, moving from one sign to the other sometime around the third week of the calendar. The monthly rituals integrate the dominant Sun sign for each month bringing the planetary undercurrent down to the surface. Embracing and working with the Sun's particular ray each month becomes an element of living and dreaming in season.

Numerology~ The Cycle of 1 through 9

Energy is also expressed numerically. Numerology assigns vibrational value to the numbers 1 through 9. As in Astrology, this numeric science describes both the positive and negative aspects of the energy's expression. Our given name at birth can be translated into a numeric formula offering insight on our chosen path through life. We can also determine the influence of particular days, months and years over the course of our lifetime.

To help us live and dream seasonally, we can work with the vibrational essence of each month. Following the Gregorian calendar the months are already assigned a numeric value, beginning with January (1) and ending with December (12, 1+2=3). Multiple digits are reduced to a single digit. November stands out because the number is 11. Numbers 11 and 22 are considered master numbers which carry intense celestial energy. Under some circumstances, the master numbers may be reduced to their single digit. To heighten our celestial awareness, November will remain an 11.

The cyclical aspect of Numerology is a reason it was chosen for inclusion in the rituals. The energy builds as it begins a cycle with 1 and completes the journey in 9. Likewise, the seasonal wheel also cycles through the natural world giving birth, life, and death. Energy expressed numerically is yet another layer to be worked consciously as we move through the calendar living and dreaming compatibly with the natural world.

Feng Shui~ Influence of Baguas on Ritual

Wind and water, as natural forces can inspire both a sense of calm and dread. Their expression is constructive or destructive. Feng Shui is a Taoist based practice dating back possibly 5,000 years. This ancient practice helps us channel the chi carried through the forces of wind and water. The intention of Feng Shui is twofold: to help us survive by locating auspicious sites for work and home and thrive by directing chi towards specific hopes and dreams.

Chi, the unifying force of the universe, is present in all things. Our homes and material possessions all contain chi which represent the natural world's base composition of masculine and feminine energy and the elemental properties of water, wood, fire, metal and earth. Their physical and metaphysical qualities influence the feel of our homes and define our relationship to the space. It's therefore possible to intentionally direct chi in our homes. The goal is to harmonize and balance our personal energy with the incoming and indwelling chi.

This electrically alive energy is also expressed through the Baguas. Baguas are physical areas in the home which represent 8 qualities of daily life each of us encounter. They are: career, knowledge & spirituality, health & family, wealth & abundance, fame & reputation, love & relationship, children & creativity, and helpful people & travel. These aspects of life correspond to the 8 trigrams of the *I Ching*, referred to as the Book of Change. The inspiration of the *I Ching* is the underpinning of the Baguas.

This ancient book suggests that a life well lived is best achieved by submitting to the natural ebb and flow of the natural world. Those on a quest for enlightenment have found the I Ching's wisdom profoundly helpful in gleaning the existential significance of life's journey. We understand how life can drop us to our knees. The storms we encounter along the way are natural occurrences. Although unpleasant and sometimes impossible to embrace, storms do offer us at the very least a reason to pause. It's in these moments when we need to stop, take a breath and then rise slowly with a resolve to live through the experience. Once weathered, we take stock and move on, stronger in resolve and purpose.

The Western School of Feng Shui orients the Baguas based on the location of the front entrance of the home. The Bagua map (included) is then placed over the floor plan of our home to identify the spatial areas in which the 8 qualities of life reside, housed within the Baguas. The map may also be used in each room using the door into the space to orient the map's placement. In ritual, we can select a Bagua that corresponds to a particular intent or goal. The Bagua can direct energy towards our goal by unifying our personal energy with the physical and spiritual energy as defined by Feng Shui to manifest our dreams. For instance, let's say we just moved to a new town and want to rebuild our social network. We may choose to focus on the health & family Bagua because of its emphasis on building a strong social circle. Interestingly, the Baguas also cycle through the seasons aiding in the turning of the wheel. For this reason the health & family Bagua was selected for one of the spring rituals. Cultivation of a strong foundation is necessary to help us weather the rainy season and life's downpours.

The Baguas will be used to help us perform tasks in preparation for the ritual and to harness the ritual's spiritual intent afterwards. If a suggested Bagua is located in an unusable space you may choose an alternative Bagua that best fits the intent.

Baguas in detail~

Ch'ien~ Helpful People & Travel (front right of entrance)

Our spiritual leaders, ancestors and mentors both living and dead are exalted in this Bagua. When we're living in the flow we have all we need to actualize our highest good. Honoring our advisors keeps them close and ready to help.

K'an~ Career (front center of entrance)

Our truest desires and purpose reside in the depths of our being. A leap of faith is required to discover what makes our soul sing. Journeying through the 'dark night of the soul' may be necessary to uncover our bliss.

Ken~ Knowledge & Spirituality (front left of entrance)

Experience is action reflected upon. Time and space allows our inner self to gather and sift through our encounters with daily life. In stillness, meaning rises to the surface as insight and knowledge gained.

Chen~ Health & Family (center left of entrance)

A sense of well being comes from a balanced life. Our inner foundation and body need work, rest and play. A strong and present circle of support helps us survive the storms of life and learn from them.

Sun~ Wealth & Prosperity (back left of entrance)

Abundance is the manifestation of our heart's desire and thus encompasses the whole myriad of life experience. Sustenance is a divine birthright. We have the power to create a full life and to pursue those things that feed the mind, body and soul.

Li~ Fame & Reputation (back center of entrance)

When the pursuit of abundance is done with integrity, the outcome benefits us all. Public recognition of our mark upon the world is not necessary for it to be known.

K'un~ Love & Relationship (back right of entrance)

Generosity begins at home. Our primary relationship is with the self. Loving ourselves honors our divinity. When all is right and true within, our significant relationships are positioned to do the same. To thine own self be true.

Tui~ Children & Creativity (center right of entrance)

Wonder and joy needn't be extinguished by maturity. Light and laughter balances the steady toil of life. Inspiration prefers a playmate to a workmate. Creative juices flow effortlessly when not weighed down.

Center or Earth~ (center)

According to Feng Shui, when the 8 qualities of life are cultivated within the home or room, balance is achieved throughout. The concept is similar to the experience of feeling grounded and centered in the flow of our lives.

Bagua Map for the Home

8 Qualities of Life

SUN Wealth, Abundance & Prosperity	LI Fame & Reputation	K'UN Love & Relationships
CHEN Health, Family & Friends	Center	TUI Children & Creativity
KEN Knowledge, Spirituality & Education	K'AN Career, Journey, & Life Direction	CH'IEN Helpful People & Travel

***************** Front of Home or Room *****************

The Western Bagua is based on the front of the property. The door opens in either

the Knowledge & Spirituality, Career, or Helpful People & Travel Bagua.

Wicca~ The Religion of the Goddess

Thus far we have explored three of the four ancient traditions: Astrology, Numerology, and Feng Shui. These branches of the Wise Hazel Tree will be used in the rituals to create a multi-textured seasonal experience. Wicca, the religion of the Goddess, is the final branch chosen from the tree of wisdom. This religion, entwined with the Mother's rich sensual bounty, will complete the seasonal flavor of the rituals.

For readers unfamiliar with Wicca it is necessary to first debunk the evil myth surrounding witches. Unfortunately, the term witch can still stir immediate misgivings and images of dark magic conjured in black, smoldering cauldrons. This perception couldn't be further from the truth. Followers of the Goddess, above all else, respect and honor the divinity of Mother Earth. We cherish and protect the Mother's inhabitants from waste, greed and abuse, the result of power's misuse. Contrary to our reputation, witches do not cast spells against another. We practice the magick of light not dark. Bewitchment through spell and charm is for good. Our creed is do what ye will and harm none.

To understand Wicca, we must acknowledge both the divine masculine (yang) and feminine (yin) energies reflected in nature. We see the divine reflection in both masculine and feminine offspring. Yet, we tend to ignore the feminine power of the universe. Our evolvement as humans away from the divine feminine has woefully tipped the scales in favor of masculine based religions. Our world needs the Mother's breath to enliven our feminine nature. The energies of yin and yang work best when in harmony with each other. Yin's receptive understanding of the world can shape the active and searching energy of yang. In the absence of yang, yin withdraws too deep into the self. In the absence of yin, yang tends to search and destroy rather than search and create. When united, both energies, equal in power have the capacity to steer our evolvement back to our roots within the natural world. The religion of Wicca acknowledges this yin and yang of spirit by worshiping both the Goddess and the God.

As the pagan wheel of life turns, Wicca honors the seasonal bounty by celebrating eight holy days called Sabbats. Four are grounded in nature's changing seasons: the winter and summer solstices and the fall and spring equinoxes. They're also known as Yule, Litha, Mabon and Ostara respectively. The other four holidays also celebrate nature's offerings and are observed in October (All Hallow's Eve), February (Candlemas), May (Beltane), and August (Lughnasadh). Each Sabbat in its own way contributes to the cycle of life, birth and death, the pagan wheel of life. The Sabbat blessings are offered as the last branch of wisdom, the final ingredient for *The Wise Hazel Tree's* brew for living in season.

Suggested
Reading

Barker, Cecily M. *Fairyopolis: A Flower Fairies Journal*. London, England: Penguin Group, 2005.

Brown, Simon. *Practical Feng Shui*. Strand, London: Wellington House, 1997.

Campbell, Florence. *Your Days Are Numbered: A Manual of Numerology for Everybody*. Marina del Rey, California: DeVorss & Company, 24th Printing, 1987.

Chocron, Daya Sarai. *Healing With Crystals and Gemstones. York Beach*, Maine: Samuel Weiser, Inc., 1986.

Chuen, Master Lam Kam. *The Personal Feng Shui Manual*. New York, New York: Henry Holt & Company, Inc., 1998.

Collins, Terah Kathryn. *The Western Guide to Feng Shui*. Carlsbad, California: Hay House, 1996.

Collins, Terah Kathryn. *The Western Guide to Feng Shui- Room to Room*. Carlsbad, California: Hay House, 1999.

Cunningham, Scott. *Wicca: A Guide For the Solitary Practitioner*. St. Paul, Minnesota: Llewellyn Publications, 1995.

Fairchild, Dennis. *Healing Homes: Feng Shui- Here & Now*. Birmingham, Michigan: WaveField Books, 1996.

Froud, Brian and Alan Lee. *Faeries*. New York, New York: Harry N. Abrams, 1978.

Froud, Brian. *Good Faeries*. New York, New York: Simon & Schuster Editions, 1998.

Gallagher, Ann-Marie. *The Wicca Bible*. New York, New York: Sterling Publishing Co., Inc., 2005.

Hall, Judy. *The Crystal Bible*. Cincinnati, Ohio: Walking Stick Press, 2003.

Hall, Judy. *The Crystal Zodiac*. New York, New York: Sterling Publishing Co., Inc., 2004.

Hay, Louise L. *You Can Heal Your Life*. Carlsbad, California: Hay House, 1987.

Jurriaanse, D. *The Practical Pendulum Book*. York Beach, Maine: Samuel Weiser, Inc., 1986.

Linn, Denise. *Sacred Space*. New York, New York: Random House, 1995.

McCoy, Edain. *Lady of the Night*. St. Paul, Minnesota: Llewellyn Publications, 1995.

McCoy, Edain. *Sabbats*. Woodbury, Minnesota: Llewellyn Publications, 10th Printing, 2006.

Myss, Caroline. *Sacred Contracts*. New York, New York: Harmony Books, 2001.

Nichols, Mike. The Eight Sabbats of Witchcraft. http://www.hermetics.org/pdf/8Sabbatsof Witchcraft.pdf

Noble, Vicki. *Motherpeace*. New York, New York: Harper & Row, Publishers, Inc., 1983.

Peschel, Lisa. *A Practical Guide to The Runes.* Woodbury, Minnesota: Llewellyn Publications, 14th Printing, 2007.

Price, Shirley. *Practical Aromatherapy.* Wellingborough, Northamptonshire, England: Thorsons Publishers Limited, 1987.

Rossbach, Sarah. *Feng Shui- The Chinese Art of Placement.* New York, New York: Penguin Books, 1983.

Rossbach, Sarah. *Interior Design with Feng Shui.* New York, New York: Penguin Books, 1987.

Rossbach, Sarah and Lin Yun. *Living Color.* New York, New York: Kodansha America, Inc., 1994.

Telesco, Patricia. *365 Goddess.* New York, New York: HarperCollins Publishers, Inc., 1998.

Thompson, Angel. *Feng Shui.* New York, New York: St. Martin's Press, 1996.

Webster, Richard. *Feng Shui for Beginners.* St. Paul, Minnesota: Llewellyn Publications, 1999.

Woolfolk, Joanna Martine. *The Only Astrology Book You'll Ever Need.* Lantham, Maryland: Scarborough House/Publishers, 1982, 1990.

Printed in the United States
By Bookmasters